DARK PSYCHOLOGY

How to Stop Being Manipulated Without Needing to Go to Therapy

(The Most Powerful Techniques of Manipulation and Methods of Persuasion)

Estella Estrada

Published by Sharon Lohan

© **Estella Estrada**

All Rights Reserved

Dark Psychology: How to Stop Being Manipulated Without Needing to Go to Therapy (The Most Powerful Techniques of Manipulation and Methods of Persuasion)

ISBN 978-1-990334-55-9

All rights reserved. No part of this guide may be reproduced in any form without permission in writing from the publisher except in the case of brief quotations embodied in critical articles or reviews.

Legal & Disclaimer

The information contained in this book is not designed to replace or take the place of any form of medicine or professional medical advice. The information in this book has been provided for educational and entertainment purposes only.

The information contained in this book has been compiled from sources deemed reliable, and it is accurate to the best of the Author's knowledge; however, the Author cannot guarantee its accuracy and validity and cannot be held liable for any errors or omissions. Changes are periodically made to this book. You must consult your doctor or get professional medical advice before using any of the suggested remedies, techniques, or information in this book.

Upon using the information contained in this book, you agree to hold harmless the Author from and against any damages, costs, and expenses, including any legal fees potentially resulting from the application of any of the information provided by this guide. This disclaimer applies to any damages or injury caused by the use and application, whether directly or indirectly, of any advice or information presented, whether for breach of contract, tort, negligence, personal injury, criminal intent, or under any other cause of action.

You agree to accept all risks of using the information presented inside this book. You need to consult a professional medical practitioner in order to ensure you are both able and healthy enough to participate in this program.

Table of Contents

INTRODUCTION 1

CHAPTER 1: WHAT IS DARK PSYCHOLOGY? 7

CHAPTER 2: BODY LANGUAGE 12

CHAPTER 3: MACHIAVELLIAN PHILOSOPHY 26

CHAPTER 4: AN IN-DEPTH LOOK AT MANIPULATION 32

CHAPTER 5: THE SUBTLE ART OF GETTING WHAT YOU WANT 40

CHAPTER 6: SUBLIMINAL INFLUENCING: PERSUASION YOU'RE NOT AWARE OF 72

CHAPTER 7: PERSUASION 98

CHAPTER 8: USING DARK PSYCHOLOGY TO MANAGE EMOTIONS 110

CHAPTER 9: WHAT MACHIAVELLIANISM IS 149

CHAPTER 10: DECEPTION- BEYOND THE LITTLE WHITE LIE 159

CHAPTER 11: UNDETECTED MIND CONTROL 171

CONCLUSION 187

Introduction

The science of psychology is one that hasn't existed for as long as many other sciences. While geology, biology, and other hard sciences have existed for hundreds or even thousands of years, psychology was born in 1874 when German physiologist Wilhelm Wundt published a manuscript outlining the connections between the body's reactions the human mind titled Principles of Physiological Psychology. This manuscript would lay the foundation for many researchers to look into the science of the human mind and people's thought process. This research path would become a branch of science all its own, and that branch would be known as psychology. Although there are now many different kinds of psychology based on methods of treatment of other researchers' perspectives, it's essential to make the distinction of the birth of science generally better to understand the idea of "dark" psychology.

The idea of dark psychology became popularized when the dark triad of human traits became a general topic. This dark triad of personality traits can be found in just about everybody. Still, the combination of the three traits—psychopathy, narcissism, and Machiavellianism—makes up the whole idea of a wrong person, in their rawest and simplest form. Research of these dark three traits can be found, especially in criminal or deviant psychology. Everyone can show signs of at least one of these traits, but they are a staple of manipulative and evil people. When the ideas of these dark psychological qualities became associated with deviance or criminal behavior, more research was done on the ideas behind what made some people deviant and what made some psychology "dark." These ideas of "dark psychology" ultimately stem from manipulation methods to convince people to lean your way or get what you want out of the people around you.

Unfortunately, there's no way for you to magically get what you want out of anyone you ask—although you can make your chances of success with certain people better by using some of these tricks, there's no guarantee or 100% success rate. There will always be some things you have to work for or go "the long way" to get. If anything, these tips and tricks are no shortcuts to get anything that you want. Still, they're ways for you to check yourself to make sure that you're also able to protect yourself from that same manipulation in addition to manipulating others. There will be many times when people try to use these tricks to get information or a favor out of you, and reading this manuscript will make those tricks less likely to work on you. And by understanding more about the dark triad of personality traits, in particular, you'll be more able to spot people with these traits easily, and you'll be able to avoid potentially dangerous or toxic people before it's too late.

In 2006, Michael Nuccitelli published his analysis of the human condition's more evil unit, titled Dark Side of The Human Consciousness Concept. In his research, Nuccitelli asserted that all humans have the ability and often the motivation to harm or victimize others. While most people don't act on these impulses, a small percentage of people that feel the desire to brutalize other people will do so based on that craving. s01% commits acts of brutalization or harm to others to fulfill some abstract sense of malice. In contrast, the whopping majority of the human race only ever acts out to achieve a purpose which they prioritize in their life. This motivation is often some attempt at the grasp of power over others or a situation in their life. The power can be literal, emotional, or spiritual. Because humans, acting under Nuccitelli's understanding of dark psychology, rarely act purely on malevolent or malicious impulses no matter how deviant or criminally attuned they are, humans are also most naturally able to do good things rather than vicious, "evil" things. When people do hateful things purely for the sake of inflicting physical or emotional harm onto others, Nuccitelli implies, they're acting as a total outlier of the majority of humanity. So, dark psychology is not the art of being evil or downright malicious. Dark psychology is very merely the unit of psychology wherein, not everything serves to understand your mind better and alleviating negative feelings. While most psychology serves the purpose of helping others, the primary directive for dark psychology is to help yourself—be able to understand people better so you can avoid negative ones, and use mind tools in able to get what you want. This is how you can use dark psychology for your benefit without turning it into a weapon.

This book will teach you everything you need to know about dark psychology's intricacies, ranging from understanding body language to how to manipulate other people. Focusing on a wide range of techniques and skills, you will learn the steps involved in taking over another person's mind and the importance of ethics. Some persuasion is relatively harmless and benefits everyone involved. Other manipulation and mind control are entirely selfish, seeking to do nothing but help the manipulator. When you understand that fine line between ethical and unethical, as well as the steps involved, you will find yourself able to influence those around you.

Chapter 1: What Is Dark Psychology?

Dark psychology can be defined as studying the human condition in its relation to the individual psychological nature to target other people as its prey. Such people are usually motivated by deviant or criminal activities without bothering about the theories of social sciences and instinctual drives. The entire humanity has this type of potentiality of victimizing their fellow human beings and other living creatures. Whereas many try to either sublimate or restrain this kind of tendency, there are still those who act upon these impulses without a second thought.

The main objective of dark psychology is to understand those perceptions, feelings, thoughts, and the subjective processing systems that lead to the predatory behavior that is contrary to the contemporary comprehension of human beings' behavior. On top of all that, the study of dark psychology also tends to assume that the deviant, criminal, and abusive nature of some human beings are all intentional and purposive. It also assumes that human beings' bestiality nature carries certain goal-oriented motivation, about 99% of the entire time. The remaining 1% is obtained from a topic that is known as Teleology.

Dark psychology also entails all the bits that make us the people we are connected to our dark side. All humanity, faiths, and cultures have this well-known proverbial disease. Beginning just from the time we are born up to the time we die, there is usually a hidden side within us. This has been defined using various names. Some have referred to this side as evil, while others have referred to it as psychopathic, deviant, and criminal. According to dark psychology, certain individuals commit these very acts and do that not for gains related to sex, money, retribution, power, or any other well-defined purpose. Some people just carry these horrid acts without a major goal. This just shows that their ends do not, in any way, justify their means. It is also a fact that certain individuals injure and violate others without any defined means. They just do that for the sake of doing so.

There are so many ways in which psychology can be of benefit to us. One of these many ways is being able to understand the full psycho-evolutionary nature of our behaviors so that we can pick our actions with more care. Human beings are usually not in control of all their actions, although they usually think they are. For instance, many of us strongly believe that we have a stable and consistent self and are even convinced that we can easily foretell our future actions. But the question that we need to ask ourselves is if we can be sure of how we will behave in the future, for instance, under very harsh pressure. Many people might be tempted to believe that we can stay calm even when in crisis.

The truth is that just a small number of us can predict how we will act under very strict conditions. This happens because of certain precepts that happen to all human beings. When we are under pressure, we experience either a fight or flight reaction. This kind of reaction evolved to aid our survival in very dangerous encounters. The flight or fight reaction also tends to shut down higher functioning when they are activated. For instance, higher brain activity is psychologically hard to run when it comes to blood sugar. Therefore, the body will conserve it.

Despite all that, this is one of the best systems for surviving any kind of mastodon attack. It can be useless in this modern-day world where we need our higher functioning when we are under a certain form of stress. To make it more understandable, each time we experience topnotch stress or are in imagined or real danger, we fail to act in certain ways or think in a straight manner.

Chapter 2: Body Language

Being able to communicate well is extremely important when wanting to succeed in the personal and professional world, but it isn't the words you say that scream. It is your body language that does the screaming. Your gestures, posture, eye contact, facial expressions, and tone of voice are your best communication tools. These can confuse, undermine, offend, build trust, draw others in, or put someone at ease.

There is many times where what someone says and what their body language says is different. Non-verbal communication could do five things:

●Substitute – It could be used in place of a verbal message.

●Accent – It could underline or accent your verbal message.

- **Complement** – It could complement or add to what you are saying verbally.

- **Repeat** – It could strengthen and repeat your verbal message.

- **Contradict** – It could go against what you are trying to say verbally to make your listener think that you are lying.

We are going to cover:

Gestures – These have been woven into our lives. You might speak animatedly; argue with your hands, point, wave, or beckon. Gestures do change according to cultures.

Facial expressions – You will learn that the face is expressive and able to show several emotions without speaking one word. Unlike what you say and other types of body language, facial expressions are usually universal.

Eye contact – Because sight tends to be our strongest sense for most people, it is an important part of Non-verbal communication. The way someone looks at you could tell you whether they are attracted to you, affectionate, hostile, or interested. It might also help the conversation flow.

Body movement and posture – Take a moment to think about how you view people based on how they hold their head, stand, walk around, and sit. The way a person carries their self gives you a lot of information. Non-verbal communication could go wrong in several different ways.

Lower Body

The arms share a lot of information. The hands share a lot more, but legs give us the exclamation point and can tell us exactly what someone is thinking. The legs could tell you if a person is open and comfortable. They could also who dominance or where they want to go.

Legs Touching

When a person is standing, they will only be able to touch their bottom or thighs. This can be done seductively or they could slap their legs as if they are saying "Let's go." It might also indicate irritation. This is when you have to pay attention to the context of the conversation. This is very important.

Pointing Feet

Look at the direction of a person's feet to see where their attention is. Their feet will always point toward what is on their mind or what they are concentrating on. Everyone has a lead foot and it all depends on their dominant hand. If a person is talking that we are interested in is talking, our lead foot will be pointing toward them. But, if they want to leave the situation, you will notice their foot pointing toward an exit or the way they want to go. If a person is sitting during the conversation, look at where their feet are pointing to see what they are truly interested in.

Smarty Pants

This is a position where someone tries to make they look bigger. They will usually be seated with their legs splayed open and leaning back. They might even spread their arms out and lock them behind their head. This is normally used by people who feel dominant, superior, or confident.

Shy Tangle

This is usually something that women do more than men. Anyone who begins to feel shy or timid will sometimes entangle their legs by crossing them under and over to try to block out bad emotions and to make they look smaller. There is another shy leg twirl that people will do when they are standing. The actual act of this movement is crossing one leg over the other and hooking that foot behind their knee as if they are trying to scratch an itch.

Upper Body

Upper body language can show signs of defensiveness since the arms could easily be used as a shield. Upper body language could involve the chest. Let's look at some upper body language.

Leaning

If someone leans forward, it will move them closer to another person. There are two possible meaning to this. First, it will tell you that they are interested in something, which could just be what you are talking about. But, this movement could also show romantic interest. Second, leaning forward could invade a person's personal space; hence, this shows them as a threat. This is often an aggressive display. This is done unconsciously by powerful people.

The Superman

Bodybuilders, models commonly use this, and it was made popular by Superman. This could have various meanings depending on how a person uses it. Within the animal world, animals will try to make themselves look bigger when they feel threatened. If you look at a house cat when they get spooked, they will stretch their legs and their fur stands on end. Humans also have this, even if it isn't as noticeable. This is why we get goosebumps. Because we can't make ourselves look bigger, we have to come up with arm gestures like putting our hands on our waist. This shows us that a person is getting ready to act assertively.

This is normal for athletes to do before a game or a wife who is nagging their spouse. A guy who is flirting with a girl will use this to look assertive. This is what we call a readiness gesture.

The Chest in Profile

If a person stands sideways or at a 45-degree angle, they are trying to accentuate their chest. They might also thrust out their chest, more on this in a minute. Women do this posture to show off their breasts and men will do this to show off their profile.

Outward Thrust Chest

If someone pushes their chest out, they are trying to draw attention to this part of their body. This could also be used as a romantic display. Women understand that men have been programmed to be aroused by breasts. If you see a woman pushing her chest out, she might be inviting intimate relations. Men will thrust out their chest to show off their chest and possibly trying to hide their gut. The difference is that men will do this to women and other men.

Hands

Human hands have 27 bones and they are a very expressive part of the body. This gives us a lot of capability to handle our environment.

Reading palms isn't about just looking at the lines on the hands. After a person's face, the hands are the best source for body language. Hand gestures are different across cultures and one hand gesture might be innocent in one country but very offensive in another.

Hand signals may be small but they show what our subconscious is thinking. A gesture might be exaggerated and done using both hands to show a point

Control

If a person is holding their hand with their palms facing down, they might be figuratively holding onto or restraining another person. This could be an authoritative action that is telling you to stop now. It might be a request asking you to calm down. This will be apparent if someone places their dominant hand on top of a handshake. If they are leaning on their desk with their palms flat, this shows dominance.

If their palms face outward toward another person, they might be trying to fend them off or push them away. They might be saying "stop, don't come closer."

If they are pointing their finger or their entire hand, they might be telling someone to leave now.

Greeting

Our hands get used a lot to greet other people. The most common way is with a handshake. Opening up the palm shows they don't have any weapons. This gets used when saluting, waving, or greeting others.

During this time, we get to touch another person and it might send various signals.

Dominance can be shown by shaking hands and placing the other hand on top. How long and how strong they shake the hand will tell you that they are deciding on when to stop the handshake.

Affection could be shown with the duration and speed of the handshake, smiles, and touching with the other hand. The similarity between this one and the dominant one could lead to a situation when a dominant person will try to pretend they are just being friendly.

Submission gets shows by placing their palms up. Floppy handshakes that are clammy along with a quick withdrawal also show submission.

Most handshakes use vertical palms that will show equality. They will be firm but won't crush and for the right amount of time so both parties know when they should let go.

Waving is a great way to greet people and could be performed from a long distance.

Salutes are normally done by the military, where a certain style is prescribed.

Holding

A person who has cupped hands shows they can hold something gently. They show delicacy or holding something fragile. Hands that grip will show desire, possessiveness, or ownership. The tighter the fist, the stronger they are feeling a specific emotion.

If someone is holding their own hands, they are trying to comfort themselves. They could be trying to restrain themselves so they will let somebody else talk. It could be used if they are angry and it is stopping them from attacking. If they are wringing their hands, they are feeling extremely nervous.

Holding their hands behind their back will show they are confident because they are opening up their front. They may hide their hands to conceal their tension. If one hand is gripping the other arm, the tighter and higher the grip, the tenser they are.

Two hands might show various desires. If one hand is forming a fist but the other is holding it back, this might show that they would like to punch somebody.

If someone is lying, they will try to control their hands. If they are holding them still, you might want to be a bit suspicious. Remember that these are just indicators and you should look for other signals.

If someone looks like they are holding onto an object like a pen or cup, this shows they are trying to comfort themselves. If a person is holding a cup but they are holding it very close and it looks like they are "hugging" the cup, they are hugging themselves. Holding onto any item with both hands shows they have closed themselves off from others.

Items might be used as a distraction to release nervous energy like holding a pen but they are clicking it off and on, doodling, or messing with it. If their hands are clenched together in front of them but they are relaxed, and their thumbs are resting on each other it might be showing pleasure.

Chapter 3: Machiavellian Philosophy

This specific character trait interests most people because it has its roots, at least in part, in a work of political philosophy written by the diplomat and political philosopher, Niccolo Machiavelli, in the Renaissance era. While imprisoned, he wrote a book detailing all the principles he deemed necessary for rulers and would be rulers to acquire and retain power. This was sent to the ruler at the time in the hopes that it would buy him some favor in the eyes of price Di Medici.

This book became the blueprint used by politicians and those who might rule over people in a broad and impactful fashion. While most people have some of these Machiavellian traits, they will seldom act on them too often. The true Machiavellian does not care about moderating these behaviors. They will, in fact, live by them as if by some philosophical code for their lives.

It is interesting to note that this is one of the easiest traits for most people to adopt and benefit from, despite being a symptom of mental illness. People can be born with this trait though, but the evidence that supports this is rare. More often than not, people high in Machiavellianism (high Machs) are more likely to have been made this way by having been subjected to a childhood that involved a cold style of parenting and everything seemed conditional at best.

Real Life Examples

High Machs, are master manipulators capable of ruining the lives of many while having the potential to teach many about those who play games of power and how to handle yourself around them. It does not matter whether one intends to learn about them out of curiosity; to deal with them in some sphere of life; or adopt some of their habits as their own to get what they want from life. These people offer a lot of wisdom to offer anyone willing to learn.

How does the High Mach operate?

Like all three of the personality types on the dark triad, the Machiavellian is often insanely charming. All that matters to them is usually that they get what they want by any means necessary. They can be terribly selfish people with very little or no sense of morality or remorse.

One of the easiest examples to conjure up of this person is the character, Iago, from Shakespeare's "Othello". High Machs, like Iago, are cunning and very manipulative, using anyone or anything to help them get the advantages they want and feel they deserve. They will cunningly operate from the shadows and show surprising amounts of patience because the end result matters more than anything else to them. The only thing that might matter as much as the end result to a High Mach, is their reputation.

Reputation to someone high in Machiavellianism, is king. There is no better way of not getting caught out as a deceiving manipulator than having a pristine reputation. Think of politicians and/or businessmen who get found out for having been involved in some scandalous affair or dodgy dealing long after they were dead or retired. These are the kinds of people who hid their sordid personas behind the impeccable reputation. Machiavellians tend to be drawn to the long game because they often consider their goals to be more important than human relationships, so they have few to no real personal attachments to hold them back.

High Machs are often so dedicated to their own interests that people around them only exist on two sides of the same coin: those who benefit me and those who do not. People are just a tool for them to use and manipulate to their own end. Get in their way though and they will deal with you ruthlessly as they have little to no remorse and are cynical by nature, not believing in any inherent goodness in people.

What can be taken away from the Machiavellian?

While most people might not be high in trait Machiavellianism, there is a lot we can learn from this leg of the dark triad. It has some elements to it that ordinary people can learn from in order to get what they want or at least live more peaceful lives where they are not constantly being taken advantage of. That last part speaks more to people who are very low on the Machiavellian scale and tend to be too 'nice' or agreeable.

The potential to build a better life in many respects is found in this part of the dark triad if one knows what to look out for and use wisely. There are many bad aspects to being a high Mach, but there are some great advantages to being willing to learn from this type of person.

Patience and reputation are among the biggest things one can take away from the Machiavellian. Loathed to investing in short cuts, the Machiavellian teaches us that patience is key when climbing the ladder of power and success.

People are also important, so learning how to pick and choose the right targets so that the rise to the top is made faster is crucial. If something underhanded must be done, then find someone to do it for you while you keep your nose clean. A good reputation will do a lot of your persuading for you.

Chapter 4: An In-Depth Look At Manipulation

When we speak about manipulation that doesn't involve force or controlling someone's finances, we are talking about psychological manipulation. Psychological manipulation is a type of social influence which, through deceptive or covert ways, influences a person's perception of the world or their behavior.

Manipulation can further be broken down into two subsets: positive manipulation and negative manipulation. Positive manipulation occurs when someone is being manipulated for their own good. An example of this would be a doctor trying to convince his patient to stop smoking. Negative manipulation is the opposite—it involves manipulating another person for ulterior motives or personal gain. An example of negative manipulation would be a salesman convincing a customer to buy a product which he knows is defective or will not be suitable for the buyer.

George Simon posits that manipulation essentially consists of two factors—the first factor being the ability to conceal aggression or negative intentions, and the second being the ability to read people. Manipulators need to be able to extrapolate the weaknesses of the person they are trying to manipulate in order to exploit them, and thus they need to be incredibly skilled in analyzing people and their motivations.

In 1996, Simon authored a self-help book titled In Sheep's Clothing: Understanding and Dealing with Manipulative People. In this book, he posited that successful manipulators usually:

●Know their victim's psychological vulnerabilities. For example, a mother will absolutely go out of her way if she thinks what she is doing will be to the benefit of her child. Similarly, if someone has a phobia of large crowds, this can be used to manipulate them into not going to a party (for example) by telling them that you expect many people to be there.

●Are ruthless. Manipulators need to be ruthless to avoid having moral qualms about influencing people in the way they do. Being unconcerned with the welfare of the person you're manipulating is par for the course.

●Have the ability to conceal their emotions and use it to their advantage. This makes sense, when you think about it. Breaking into tears during a formal debate in high school would be a terrible idea and would influence absolutely nobody; however, breaking into tears while asking someone for a loan would definitely work to your advantage, as you would be forcing the person to empathize with you.

Simon went even further, eventually studying the techniques that manipulators use to influence people. These methods range from lying, to feigning confusion and innocence, to playing the victim, and, of course, seduction.

Simon isn't the only psychologist who has studied manipulators and their ways. Harriet Braiker was a clinical psychologist who rose to fame in the year 2000 with her book, The Disease to Please, in which she discussed how easily influenced people-pleasers are. In her 2004 novel, Who is Pulling the Strings, she further elaborated on the concept of manipulation—but this time, the focus was on the manipulators themselves. Braiker identified four distinctive ways in which manipulators influence people:

Punishment. This doesn't mean punishment like a parent would punish a child by, for example, grounding them. Manipulators use social punishment to ensure they can exert their influence over others. The most common form of social punishment is the silent treatment, whereby they exclude the person from events or driving a wedge between the person and their friends or family.

Positive reinforcement. To put it simply, this is flattery. Manipulators may try to get their way by showering the person they wish to influence with compliments, or by doing nice things for them (like bringing them coffee to work). Positive reinforcement may be as seemingly insignificant as a smile or a pat on the back, or as grandiose as drawing public attention to the person the manipulator wishes to influence.

Negative reinforcement. Negative reinforcement, despite its misleading name, does not involve punishment. Instead, it's a different type of reward. A manipulator who is using negative reinforcement might say, "You don't have to come to the meeting tomorrow if you drive me to the mall today." In this way, the manipulator frees the person they wish to influence from doing something which they do not wish to do by, essentially, forcing them to accept the manipulator's alternative.

Traumatic one-time learning. This involves the manipulator making such an impact on the person he or she wishes to manipulate that no further reinforcement or punishment is necessary. An example of this would be an outburst of anger so immense that the person on the receiving end does not even consider disobeying.

All of the above methods in which manipulators influence people require one common trait: remorselessness. And the least remorseful of them all? The psychopath. Psychopathy is a mental disorder characterised by a lack of remorse or empathy, extreme manipulativeness, antisocial behavior, and egotism. Psychopaths are master manipulators, and thus, despite their less than stellar reputation, they are fantastic role models to mirror in order to master the art of manipulation. Robert Hare and Paul Babiak theorized that psychopaths operate by manipulating people through a three-phase approach.

The first phase is known as the assessment phase. During this phase, the psychopath chooses the person they plan to manipulate. They keep an eye out for traits like status, wealth, and influence— seldomly going after someone who has nothing to offer them.

The second phase is the manipulation phase, during which the psychopath carefully crafts the persona which the person they want to manipulate will come to know. Once this 'mask' has been created, the psychopath can begin eliciting anything they want from the now very willing, trusting victim.

The third and final phase is called the abandonment phase. After the psychopath has gained all they wanted to gain from the person they've manipulated, they simply drop the mask and exit the victim's life. As soon as the person is no longer gainful to the psychopath, the psychopath will see no reason to maintain a relationship with them.

Chapter 5: The Subtle Art Of Getting What You Want

Persuasion isn't always easy to do. The people you want to persuade have the right of free choice. There will be other options they can take, leaving your option behind.

We see it in advertising all the time. You have so many different types of products to choose from that it makes picking just one a difficult task. So the makers of all products on the market today must persuade you to buy only their product.

Think about all the different types of soda there are in the market today. Each company has its own unique way of persuading the drinkers of soda to buy their drink. "It's fizzier than all the rest."

Who wouldn't want the fizziest of all the sodas?

Maybe someone with tummy issues.

So, there's another company that has thought about that and they try to persuade buyers in another way. "Our soda is the smoothest of them all."

Yes, a smooth taste is always good except if you're a kid who likes to astonish his senses. Then the company has to persuade that kid to buy their soda. "Your taste buds won't know what hit 'em when you drink our soda."

There are those who don't want any caffeine in their soda. So, the company has an idea to persuade those soda drinkers. "All the taste and none of the caffeine of our competitors' sodas."

But what if someone wants more caffeine? Companies had to come up with how to persuade those people too. "Your morning routine just got better with Hyper-speed soda with three times the caffeine of any other brand."

With so many choices out there, persuasion has never been more important. Learning how to get people to buy your product, vote the way you want them to, or think that way you need them to think, is an essential piece of knowledge everyone needs in this day and age.

Brandishing Anger

More so used in politics, brandishing anger is a technique that's meant to hit you at your core.

Take this example:

Mack is running for president of the United States. And he's angry with the current president. So, he needs you to get angry with him, so you'll vote for him and not the man he's so angry with. "You can't sit back and just allow him to keep on running our country into the ground! You've got to do something, and it has to happen right now! There is no time to wait! How will you look your children in their little faces, knowing that you never even tried to make their futures better by voting for me, the best man to take over the White House?"

As you can see here, he's mad and he's letting you know that he and your kids will be so mad at you if you don't vote for him and get the other guy out of office. He's using anger to persuade you to do as he wants you to.

Bandwagon Effect

Mack's no fool either. He didn't get to where he is by being unprepared. So, he's brought along his bandwagon to help persuade you further to cast your vote for him. "Look who I have here with me today. My elite supporters. You all know Josh from his many movie roles that have won him many Academy Awards. And who can forget about Manny's Pulitzer? He's a staunch supporter that anyone would be admired for following. We've got an awesome group here, people. It would make us all very happy to have you all join us in this great endeavor. Come, join us, the nation's best and brightest leaders."

Now, who wouldn't want to join that nation's best and brightest? And Josh, the Academy Award-winning actor is so handsome too. Who knows, maybe you'll end up working at a rally together if you join team Mack for the presidency?

Lying

Pretty much every politician anywhere has been accused of lying at one time or another. That's only because they've all lied at one time or another.

As I pointed out before, we all lie at least a few times each day. If you're a politician who is talking as much as you can to get into the office you're seeking, then you probably lie a heck of a lot more than the rest of us do.

So, getting caught in a lie isn't a thing that actually worries you. You know it will happen and you're prepared for that day.

A reporter raises his hand in the crowd in front of Mack. "Yes, Robbie the reporter?"

"Mack, you said in the last rally that you've been married for ten years. But I have done my research and that's not true at all. See, you were married for a matter of six months to a woman named Pam when you were fresh out of high school. If you add the time you've been married to your current wife, Arlene, to the time you were married to Pam, you've got eleven years in all."

Mack is ready to admit his lie. "Yes, you caught that, did ya, Robbie. Yes, I was briefly married to my high school sweetheart. We're still great friends by the way. And the reason that I don't count that time as being married is that – if you would've researched just a tad bit more –

you would've found that that marriage was annulled, making it not count."

"Oh," Robbie the reporter says with a bit of embarrassment. "Sorry about that, Mack. Go on, you were saying?"

Mack was ready with his rebuttal and never even blinked an eye when confronted.

Using Guilt

Who doesn't know that using guilt to get what you want actually works? Anyone can pull this off too. From a little kid to an elderly person, we all know how to use this great tactic when we need to.

It's like we were all born with this innate sense to help us get the things we want.

Take Johnny for instance. Johnny is six years old and he would love nothing more than to get a video game system like the ones his friends have. "Aw, come on, Dad. All the guys have one."

"Those things cost a fortune, Johnny," Dad exclaims as he puts down his newspaper. "Plus, you have to be careful with them or they can break. The last thing I want to see is something that cost me a ton of money, lying broken in the trash bin. So, for the tenth time, no. You can't have one of those things yet. You're just too young for that kind of responsibility."

Johnny puts on the puppy dog eyes as he holds his hands in front of him. "But, Dad, I will be the most careful I've ever been with anything in my entire life. If you give me that one thing, then I will never ask for another thing again as long as I live."

"Yeah?" His father grins. "So, if I get you this machine, you won't ask me for a car when you're sixteen? You won't ask me to rent you a tuxedo when you have your high school graduation? You won't ask me for even one Christmas or birthday present? And how about Easter and Halloween? You won't ask me to buy you a costume so you can go trick or treat with your friends and your brothers and sister? You won't ask me for an Easter basket so you can put the eggs you find in it?"

"Are you serious right now, Dad?" Johnny can't believe his father would go that far.

"Sure, I'm serious right now, son. You've got to think about what you say to me. Saying that if I get you this one thing then I won't have to get you anything else, just isn't true." Johnny's dad sees a lesson here. "Although you don't mean to, you're intentionally lying to me. And that just to drink their bottlehurts, son."

Johnny can tell that something is shifting in their roles within this very important conversation and he can't let that happen. "Well, I am sorry. I didn't know that I was lying to you. I wouldn't do that to you,

Dad. But you should know that my friends are the same age and they all have gaming systems that their parents all trust them with. That makes me feel like you think they're smarter than me."

Johnny's dad never meant to make his son feel that way. "Son, I didn't mean to make you feel bad. But, maybe their parents just aren't as aware of the fact that their kids are too young to be trusted not to break such an expensive item. I'm sure one of them will break their game very soon."

"What?" Johnny's eyes bug out. "You would wish that on my friends, Dad? How could you? I was just asking if you could find it in your heart to get me a gaming system. I never thought you would turn on my poor friends like this. I'm sorry I even brought it up to you now that I know how you are. I would never - not ever – wish anything bad for your friends, Dad. Like what if I said that I know that soon your buddy next door will wreck that sports car he just bought? How would that make you feel?"

"Well, pretty good, actually. That guy is too old to be driving a Corvette."

"Shame on you, Dad. Shame, shame, shame." Johnny wags his finger at his father. That man deserves that car. He's worked his whole entire life and all he wanted was to get to buy himself a car like that before he died. Shame on you, Dad."

Johnny's father is left dumbstruck. And he begins to reflect on himself. "You know what?"

"What, Dad?" Johnny crosses his arms over his chest as he waits to see what his father has to say.

"Maybe I'm saying no to you out of jealousy. I never got a game system until I was old enough to buy my own. Go get your shoes on. I'm taking you to get one right now."

Johnny runs off, shouting how much he loves his father. And not an ounce of guilt is felt by the kid for playing his father like that either.

Persuasion

We've all heard these words, 'Can I persuade you?'

Me, being me, I always say back, "No, you may not?" But I'm a real piece of work, so anyone who knows me expects that to come out of my mouth.

But if you really want to know how to get what you want, then you will leave out the actual words that let the person know that you are about to mentally manipulate them into doing what you want them to.

Andy was looking for a new car. He knew that he wanted a great deal and would be taking the cheapest car on the lot that very day. And the thing was that the salesman knew Andy was going to leave there with a car that very day because Andy had made the mistake of telling him that.

So, Leo, the salesman needs to make more commission from the sale that the cheapest car there won't bring him. Persuasion begins to play. "Yes, that is our cheapest car, Andy. And it's an okay car. But let me ask you this. Will this car last a whole year before it needs lots of expensive repairs, costing you even more money down the road to keep it running?"

It sounds to Andy like Leo is trying to give him good advice. "So, what are you saying, Leo? Should I look at something that will last longer?"

"Now, that is all up to you. I ain't one of these pushy salesmen like the rest of the guys here on the lot. I just like to help my customers get the best deal they can for the money they got."

"And I would appreciate your sage advice, Leo." Andy feels lucky that he got such a great man to help him buy his first car.

That's another thing Leo knows about Andy since he told him that as well. "Being that this is your first car, Andy, I'd hate for you to get into something with nothing but problems. Now, let me show you what I think would work for you. And mind you, it will cost a bit more, but I've got a humdinger of a great deal for you on how you can pay this car out."

Andy's surprised and pleased. "Do you mean that you can get me financed, Leo?"

"In-house is our specialty here at Gotta Have it Motor Company. You can just give us what you came here with as the down payment and then I'll write up a finance deal for you, and you'll only be charged fifty percent interest."

"Fifty sounds high to me." Andy is seeing a downside to Leo's idea.

"You should always ignore the interest charge. It's not like it will ever affect your relationship with your car. And your payment will still be affordable," Leo advises him.

"For how long, are we talking here?" Andy had to ask, knowing that he's already got some bills to pay out of the paycheck he earns from flipping burgers down at Quickie Burger.

Waving his hand as if waving away some pesky mosquitos, Leo lets him know it's not so long, "Sixty months is all." Leo knows when you use the smaller unit of time of a month over the larger unit of time of saying a year, then you can hook people a lot more easily. "Sixty payments is all you will have to make to become the owner of this car." He opens the door of a gently used Chevy Camaro. "Look at this beauty. Now, this is what every eighteen-year-old wants to be driving. Am I right?"

"I can't afford this." Andy knows this is just too good to be true. "The payments will be way too high."

"You tell me what's more important to you and I'll help you find the right car for you." Leo taps his chin as he seems to be thinking. "Is it more important to you to get great gas mileage, or pay a lower payment on a car?"

"Um, well, both kind of." Andy isn't sure where the guy is going with this.

"Okay, well then you should know that this car gets the best gas mileage out of all the cars we have on this lot right now. So, you might pay a little bit more per month but in the end, you will save it at the pumps." Leo smiles as if he's solved the kid's problems.

"And what happens if I can't come up with the payment at times?" Andy had to wonder about that.

"Not a problem in the least, Andy. See, we'll just come to pick the car up and bring it back here, keeping it here until you can pay if that doesn't take too long. We can't keep something sitting her forever. And lots of people will be ogling this yellow beauty. You probably wouldn't want to miss any payments and risk someone else buying your little beauty."

Andy looks at the sports car. "It is a beauty. And my girlfriend would love it if I came to pick her up in this."

"Oh, you will have her eating out of the palm of your hand if you take this thing to pick her up in. Eating out of the palm of your hand! So, how about a test drive?"

"Man, I shouldn't." Andy's getting a little apprehensive about the whole thing. He never went there to get himself wrapped up in payments. He wanted to pay cash for a car and get going.

Pulling the keys to the car out of his pocket, Leo tosses them to Andy. "Come on, let's take a spin. You drive. I'll show you how the stereo works while you take us on a cruise. You can see how the ladies on the street react to you behind the wheel of this beast."

"Yeah. What could a little drive hurt?"

The answer to that is well known by most of us. It can make you fall in love so hard with a car that paying only sixty payments doesn't sound so hard for you to do. You have to work for love, and you love this car. All thanks to Leos' ability to use persuasion without you ever knowing a thing about it.

Dissuasion

As easy as it is to use the power of persuasion, it's also easy to use the power of dissuasion. For this little scene, we will pick up with Andy and Leo right where we left off.

When the two got back to the lot, there sat Andy's father, waiting for them to return. He's all smiles as they get out of the car. "Hey, Andy. I noticed how long it was taking you and thought I'd come on up here to help you make a decision, buddy."

"Well, Dad, I think I've made on. This is it. This is my first car." Andy pats the hood of the car that has a bit of smoke coming out of it.

"What's that smoke about?" Andy's dad asks Leo.

"Leo, sir." He extends his hand to Andy's father. "Great to meet ya."

"Ray." He shakes the salesman's hand. "So, the smoke? What's up with that?"

"I think it's a little oil that might've spilled while we were filling it up. That's all. With the swipe of a cloth, it'll be nothing."

"Let's pop the hood, shall we. I wanna get a gander at my boy's first-ever engine." Ray reaches into the driver's side, popping the hood.

The smoke really billows out as he opens the hood. Andy waves the smoke out of his face. "Wow, there must be a whole bunch of oil that spilled when you were filling it, Leo."

"Yeah, I guess so." Leo puts his hands into his pockets, rocking back and forth, as he tries to figure out how he's going to persuade the kid's old man into letting him buy the heap of crap.

"Well, Andy," his dad says. "I think the first thing you should ask here is why oil is having to be put into this car in the first place. You know, ask if there's a leak or something."

"Oh, yeah." Andy looks at Leo. "So, is there a leak?"

"Not that I'm aware of." Leo knows there's one. "We like to make sure all the oil levels are topped off each morning is all. One of the mechanics must've just spilled some on the engine is all. I can have them get that all cleaned up while we get to the paperwork. Not a problem at all."

"Well, hold up there, Leo," Ray says. "I'm sure Andy has more he'd like to ask you before you put in too much effort on this deal. Right son?"

"Um, yeah sure, Dad." Andy looks around the car and finds something a little odd. "Um, why is the paint on the inside of the car door red and the car is yellow on the outside, Leo."

"Paint job, obviously." Leo knows the car has been in a wreck. It was totaled by the insurance company and his boss bought it at a salvage yard. "Guess the last owner liked yellow more than red. No biggie. Lots of people paint their cars."

Andy looked at his father. "Is that right, Dad?"

"I've had ten cars in my life," his dad says. "Never painted any one of them. See, son, a paint job can also mean there has been damage to the car. Let's take a look at the inside of the car for a minute."

Andy pointed out a torn seat cover in the back. "I saw this, but Leo said a little needle and thread could stitch this up."

"Yeah, so why haven't they done that if that's the case?" Ray asked. "Have you asked to see the vehicle's maintenance record?"

"Didn't know I could ask that." Andy turned to Leo. "Can I see that?"

"You sure could," Leo said with a smile. "If the owner who sold it to us had left it in the car. Sorry. But we can get to the paperwork if you're ready."

The look in his father's eyes told Andy that as much as he wanted the car, his dad thought it was a bad deal. "You know, Leo. I think I'm going to hold off. I'll save a little more money so I can buy something else outright a little later. I really don't want payments."

Ray claps Andy on the back. "I think you're right about doing that, son. Damn proud of you. You do have a good head on your shoulders."

Leo has to do something. He hadn't sold a car in days. And he's not about to miss out on making at least a little. "Well, what about the first car I showed you. We can still do that deal. That's a cash out the door price I gave you for that."

Andy looks at his Dad who once again, gives him that look that says it's a bad idea. "Naw. Thanks, Leo. I'll see you around."

Using the power of dissuasion, Andy's father has saved Andy tons of car trouble in the future.

Bribery

There is no parent in the world who hasn't used bribery to get their kids to do something.

Mother's beg their kids to eat their vegetables. "Come on, Lacy, eat your peas. They're good for you."

"No! Yucky," the three-year-old screams as she shakes her head.

So, Mom resorts to bribery. "If you take one bite of these peas, then we will go down to the ice cream shop and you can get any flavor that you want."

With wide eyes, Lacy opens her mouth and Mom has won. Or has she?

You Scratch My Back – I'll Scratch Yours

This may have come from caveman times. I can see one man having a terrible case of the fleas in the bushy hair covering his back. He can't reach the itch and has to go ask another caveman who seems to have an itch he can't scratch too.

In so many grunts and hand gestures, he gets the other caveman to see that they can both get their itches taken care of if they work together.

This technique for getting what you want has evolved quite a bit. And like anything else, it's been used for evil more than a time or two. Politicians use this technique on a daily basis nowadays.

Blackmail

Blackmail is a technique that can actually go from something a little bad to do to a person to something that is considered to be a crime and a punishable offense.

So, you can see a lame blackmailing scheme here. Jana is taking a nap and when her kid doesn't let her sleep, she resorts to blackmailing her. "Hey, you better go lay down and take your own nap or I'll tell your daddy that you didn't take it and he won't take you for ice cream after dinner."

And then you have a criminal offense. "So, you will say that you murdered that man, or I will kill your entire family, Frank. Got it?"

There are many shades of grey with this tactic for getting what you want.

Ultimatum

I don't know about you, but when some idiot thinks they're going to give me an ultimatum and I'll fall for it, I leave them empty-handed.

The whole, you can do this or this and nothing else scam is a real turn off. But so many people fall for it, that it keeps on happening.

Dave is about to dish out a couple of things Linda can do. "So, you can clean the house and I won't scream and yell at you, or you can clean the house with me screaming and yelling at you."

Now, a smart person would give him a quick answer to that. "Or you can clean your own damn mess cause it was you who made it in the first place. I'll be next door, watching television with the neighbors. Let me know when you're done."

Hidden Agenda

The hidden agenda strategy can be pulled off without anyone being the wiser of this nifty little trick of getting what you want. The key here is not to let too much get out about what you really want.

"So, I've got this golf club set that's just taking up space in my closet. Would you like to have it, Wilma? You could give it to your husband as a gift."

"Won't your husband be angry that you gave away his clubs, Lola?" Wilma's not sure she wants to be involved in that mess. "I don't want Chester to be playing golf and have Harry come at him like a tiger when he sees him using his clubs."

"Oh, that won't happen. Harry knew I was gonna clean out the closet. He won't be mad at Chester." But Lola knows that Harry loves those clubs and he would hate for her to give them away.

"I don't know. I don't want to get in the middle of anything bad." Wilma knows that the couple has a tumultuous relationship.

"Well, I'm gonna give them to someone, or I'm gonna put them in a dumpster somewhere. Either way, give them to your husband or not. I'm getting my closet cleaned out." Wilma is set on getting rid of the clubs her husband loves so much.

"Well, if you're just gonna throw them out, then sure I'll take them. Chester will be pretty happy with a free set of clubs." She's feeling okay with taking them now that she knows they would've been turned into trash.

Lola takes the clubs worth thousands of dollars and gives them to her friend. "There you go. Now I've got to clean up the rest of the closet. Thanks, Wilma. Bye now." Lola has more she has to get rid of but didn't want to ask her friend to take too many of her husband's things or she might get suspicious.

Lola had an agenda. She'd caught Harry cheating on her and now she's going to get rid of the things he loves the most, starting with the golf clubs and ending with her.

Key Takeaways

There are many ways to get what you want. Each tactic above can be used in both good and bad ways.

Using Anger.

Getting people on your bandwagon.

Lying.

Using guilt.

Using persuasion and dissuasion.

Lying to get what you want.

Bribing others to get what you want from them.

Scratching backs to get yours scratched too.

Using blackmail against others.

Having hidden agendas.

Giving others ultimatums.

It's up to you how you use these techniques.

And now you can spot them when they're being used on you.

Exercises

You find someone flattering you for absolutely no good reason as you aren't dressed up in any way take and you actually look kind of tacky. What do you do?

Someone you know asks you to do something that you consider to be immoral. When they tell you that you will do it or they will do something really bad to you or someone else, what is that called?

If you have a reason you want someone to do something, that is called having a what?

You come home to find the place a wreck and ask your kids to clean up their mess. They give you a lot of trouble doing it. Then you tell them that they will get to go to the movies if they get the house cleaned up. What is that tactic called?

Chapter 6: Subliminal Influencing: Persuasion You're Not Aware Of

Information overload is becoming a global epidemic as we are constantly bombarded with various types of news each and every day. Being well-informed is important, but unfortunately much of the information that reaches us is either trivial or insignificant. However, that's not nearly as worrying as the kind of material we are absorbing daily. It is believed so-called 'Subliminal Influencing' is carried out on us by political parties, major corporations, marketing companies, governments, via social media apps and through pop videos among other things.

'Priming' is a well-known psychological effect which explains that by encountering a certain stimulus it will trigger related ideas in the mind. Because this one thing was activated, it influences other psychological processes related to it, which can go on to influence our desires or the choices we make.

This can work in either a positive or negative way. We can 'prime' ourselves for positive action by labeling our daily tasks in an extravagant and exciting way. Instead of simply 'exercising', you can tell yourself you will be spending an hour 'sculpting an amazing body'. Although the task is essentially the same, you have primed yourself to be more excited to do it by re-wording it into a more interesting and stimulating way. Priming can also be used in a negative context. You may be preparing for a regular meeting with your boss but prior to the meeting he sends you an e-mail titled URGENT and highlights within the e-mail that this will be an 'important' meeting. Now you have been primed to perhaps fear something you otherwise weren't too concerned about.

Psychological research has shown just how easily people are influenced by the world and people around them. We think we are this independent person who makes all their own choices themselves. When in actual fact we take unconscious direction our environment which is continuously controlling our sublte behaviors. One study discovered that if people can smell cleaning liquid 'in the air' they're more likely to tidy up. Or when people spotted a briefcase, they were likely to be competitive. We can even be influenced by simply catching a glimpse of certain words such as 'support' or 'helpful'; seeing these words makes us more likely to cooperate with others. These things occur without us ever realizing what's going on.

This is not deliberate mind control or manipulation but something that is quite natural. This shows how our unconscious buttons are pressed from everyday things.

Hidden Messages

Stressful jobs and long working hours mean that most people sprawl out on the couch in front of the TV or surf the Internet for many hours as soon as they get home. Both these pastimes help with relaxation; however, is believed that when the mind is relaxed, it is much more susceptible to subliminal persuasion and more likely to take in external messages subconsciously.

What happens while watching television (or anything else relaxing), is that brain waves transfer from a beta frequency (alert state of mind) to an alpha frequency (relaxed state of mind). When alpha waves predominate, the brain becomes highly receptive to suggestions. This is the state of mind which hypnotists try to put their subjects into before introducing persuasive suggestions.

Subliminal influencing is thought to be concealed within messages behind benign audio, images and video footage. Such messages, are alleged to be camouflaged into the background of such stimulii and therefore not easily discernible. However, they influence us because, the subconscious mind is still able to detect them.

For many years people have feared that an image flashed on the screen which they didn't notice had the power to make them purchase a particular item. But is this even possible? You may wonder how long something has to be presented to us before we can detect it? This duration is said to be around 0.003 seconds, which is too quick for most of us to consciously pick up.

Some believe these hidden messages are controlling us by appealing to our unconscious desires. By supposedly influencing our perceptions through commercial advertising we are propelled into buying the latest new gadget or fashion accessory or having our voting decisions swayed via political propaganda. The understanding of such phenomena is that such messages are carefully manufactured to trigger people emotionally. Since humans are primarily feeling beings, appealing to their emotions (in theory) would make us more susceptible to influence.

Subliminal influence is similar to auto-suggestion or hypnosis wherein the subject is encouraged (or induced) to be relaxed so that suggestions can be directed to deeper parts of their mind where they can have the desired effect. Psychologists have even gone as far as to state that 'the unconscious mind is incapable of the critical refusal of hypnotic or subliminal suggestions'.

If this type of subliminal programming is, in fact, possible, then once an idea is planted into the subconscious, it would be very hard to get overide. Once it's stored there, the conscious thinking part of the mind doesn't have direct access to it. This is one of the reasons why some people nowadays avoid watching TV. Although most of us do so as it helps us relax, others believe we're being indoctrinated to act or live in a certain way and that a mass but delicate hypnosis is being conducted on the populations of the Earth.

The idea of subliminal advertising was introduced back in 1957, when a study was published by James Vicary and Frances Thayer who made the claim that when the words 'Drink Coca-Cola' and 'Eat popcorn' were subliminally presented to people watching a film, it increased sales of popcorn and coca cola by 18% and 58%, respectively. Once studies like this captured people's imagination they started to become worried they were being 'controlled' or influenced into buying certain products or voting for certain politicians. The fear was further compounded when people realized they were helpless against this sort of influencing and had no way of preventing it. Later on, it came out that Vicary and Thayer had manufactured the whole idea to promote their advertising and marketing agency. Later studies actually found that subliminal advertising wasn't as powerful as people had once anticipated. However, many remain convinced they're being influenced subliminally through television, radio, and advertising.

Since then, other studies have proven we're somewhat susceptible to subliminal influence. A later study showed that when words which related to being thirsty were subliminally presented to thirsty people, they actually drank more. Other studies supported this notion, such as customers were more likely to buy German wine from a store if German music was playing in the background and Italian wine if Italian music was playing. When the customers were asked afterward about their purchases they didn't even mention the music and were for the most part unaware of its influence.

So why was previous evidence shown to be unfounded yet other evidence proved that subliminal influencing does in fact work? There are two main factors to consider here. Firstly, for subliminal influence to have an impact, it must resonate with the current goals or needs of the individual. This is seen in the study of people who were subliminally influenced when they were thirsty, which led them to drink more. Secondly, any subliminal influence needs to be indirect and outside of our awareness to have an impact. For instance, the customers who heard the German or Italian music and then made purchases, as a result, weren't being directly influenced. But flashing the words 'drink Coca-Cola' or 'eat popcorn' are direct and it seems there are not as effective. It was later discovered that if the people buying the wine were made aware that their choices were influenced by the background music, they would have been more likely to purchase a different wine. It seems that even though we are susceptible to subliminal influence, we certainly don't like it. Another example showed that in restaurants where fast paced music was played, customers eat faster, and restaurants had a higher turnover rate of customers. The tempo of the music was influencing people to get moving.

We shouldn't be overly concerned about ads making us buy things we don't want, or making us vote for political parties we hate. At the most, they can make us buy things we are already inclined to purchase or vote for a party we already had some interest in. It's unlikely we could ever be influenced into doing specific things against our will. Such ads can have an effect but not powerfully enough. But, we are susceptible to subliminal influence when it is presented in the right way and time. Next time you're out shopping pay attention to your immediate surroundings and notice if there's anything which might be influencing your buying decisions.

It is worth mentioning that subliminal influencing is not only about exploitation. People do use it for self-help purposes, to help them manage health, lose weight, stop smoking, improve self-esteem, develop good habits, overcome fears and the like.

Media Manipulation

Media is a very powerful tool for influencing mass thinking and can work in a number of ways depending upon what needs to be achieved. As discussed, it can't make us do specific things. But it does have the power to generally push us into a certain direction or way of thinking. Once whole populations are moving in the same direction, momentum is gained and reversing it can become very difficult. A person's identity can be profoundly influenced by a set of social influence techniques where a 'new identity' is purposefully created – which teaches us to be dependent on the leader or group ideology. The person, therefore, cannot think for him or herself but believes otherwise.

Big corporations and governments are believed to be amongst the biggest users of various sophisticated, technological and psychological methods of influencing our minds and psychology.

- <u>Education</u>

In many countries (in the East and West), education is used to ensure next generations will be obedient and controlled in order to fit into the current model of society. This is healthy to a certain degree, but some argue it is taken too far. Most education systems follow the same general principles: Individualism is discouraged over group thinking; the need for obedience and dependency is endorsed; only government-approved sources of information are used; propaganda is used extensively; alternative belief systems are painted negatively or disregarded; feelings such as homesickness, depression or resentment are blocked; students are encouraged to follow ideas that the government and society approves of such as committing to long-term education (i.e. university) – 'if they don't want to fail'.

– Sports, politics, religion

A system where the inherent tribal tendencies of humans are exploited by encouraging them to cooperate and unite by forming teams, so to direct their collective focus toward domination and winning.

– TV and mass media

TV and mass media enable some of the most successful methods of spreading (mis)information, promoting fear, impending chaos (our nation is under threat....), and using uncertainty to sell (who knows if you'll have a job next year, go on your dream vacation now....).

The majority of TV programs and media outlets (newspapers, magazines, news channels) are produced by a few mega-corporations which monitor what we watch, hear and read. Not only do they present the news they want us to hear, but they also distract people by preoccupying their minds with trivia like celebrity scandals and sports news.

These are just a few techniques used by the powerful to influence populations to move and think in the way they desire.

As the famous human rights activist Malcolm X once put it, 'The media's the most powerful entity on earth. They have the power to make the innocent guilty and to make the guilty innocent, and that's power. Because they control the minds of the masses'.

8 most common ways of media manipulation:

➤ Distracting the public

This technique relies on using nationalism or inspiring fear and hatred towards a foreign country or towards a particular group. Populations can be induced into fearful states by separating them into groups and making them appear different from other groups. The individuals then naturally look for any differences between themselves and the opposing group which works to separate them even further. This makes masses of people easier to control which helps serve the agenda of those trying to gain power. This tactic is usually deployed on the basis of religion, culture or race.

➤ Distraction by major events

Commonly known as a 'smokescreen', this technique consists of making the public focus its attention on something apparently interesting, but which serves to make sure we don't focus what is really important going on at that moment. Often times the propagandist doesn't want our focus on something which goes against their agenda.

➤ Guilt by association

When the media wants to destroy a person's character publicly they will somehow associate them to something the masses would be horrified with. Or, connect the individual to some law-breaking person, organization or action.

➤ Just a little poison

This implies slowly administering poison (lies) about someone, while at the same time writing about good things related to the same person. The human mind naturally tends to focus and remember the shocking and bad things. As the saying goes, 'it can take years to build a good reputation but only 5 minutes to ruin it'.

➤ Make it funny

If they can't destroy someone, the media may try to at least make people look ridiculous, by showing photos of someone's bad side, where they look stupid, ugly, wrinkled, overweight etc. The opposite is also true, if the media wants to support someone, they'll show photos where that person looks handsome, beautiful, photogenic and dignified.

➤ Making sandwiches

If they can't openly attack someone, the media publishes articles which are not entirely bad but which instead carry a bad tone. They may add some good (true) things about the person, but they make sure the article starts and closes with negativity and doubt. This is usually enough to make the public suspicious. We naturally focus more at the beginning and the end of any stimulus.

☐ Stacking the experts

This is a technique often used in TV panel debates. Participants are carefully chosen beforehand but in such a way that the obvious disbalance is made to look balanced. For example, they invite several members who have similar views, but just one member of an opposing viewpoint whom they would like to discredit. No matter how strong this participant is on their own, they stand little chance of winning such a debate.

➤ Repetition makes true

Incessant repetition of a lie eventually registers as truth in the mind of the masses. Mass hysteria can be created by repeatedly reporting the dangers of some microbe infesting humans which can take over the world which can leave populations in tones of panic.

As Joseph Goebbels, Adolf Hitler's propaganda minister said, 'If you repeat a lie often enough, it becomes the truth.'

Subliminal Persuasion Techniques

Subliminal persuasion is a way of getting others to agree with you without openly suggesting anything and without them ever noticing that you're trying to persuade them.

Good persuaders have a knack of communicating with a person's subconscious mind so they use a series of techniques without the other person ever realizing it.

➤ Give them what they want

Get people believing it was THEIR idea. Repeat what they're saying pretending you agree with the idea, and then about how you'll achieve what they want. People, like being right and feeling appreciated, so, will gladly go along with what you say you'll do, all the time pretending it was them who suggested it. For instance, you may want to go to a particular restaurant with a work colleague but it's their turn to decide where to eat. So, you may ask them what they feel like eating? Regardless of their response, a skilled manipulator will direct the questioning to take them to the outcome they desire.

➤ Associate yourself with good things

Make sure your clients (or whomever you're trying to persuade) feels good about meeting with you. Meet them in a pleasant environment. If possible, always negotiate over lunch in a nice restaurant and foot the bill. After a couple of pleasant experiences, they'll come to associate you with good things, while becoming agreeable and more open to meeting with you in future. We can take this tactic even further by engineering our social media feeds to promote certain ideals which the other party views as favorable. For example, a teenager trying to create attraction with his crush might post images of himself attending the concert of a band which his crush adores. Through this, she will associate her admirer with something she sees as good therefore viewing him in a more favorable light also.

➤ Establish rapport

Probably the most widely used yet simple persuasion techniques - Making others feel at ease in your presence. Rapport can be built by finding what you share in common with the person you're trying to influence. This is a tactic commonly used in consumer sales. Finding commonalities makes people feel 'we are similar to them', allowing them to naturally open up to us. Once someone lets their guard down, they become much easier to figure out.

Getting to know the person you're trying to influence will help them develop a degree of trust in you. By showing we trust them, they are more likely to reciprocate this by trusting us. However, be prepared to play various roles with the people you're interacting with. Sometimes you'll need to act like you're below them, sometimes their equal and sometimes an authority figure. Quickly acknowledging the other person's personality and character allows us to slip into one of these three roles more effectively.

Once you have chosen what position to take, pay closer attention and have a genuine interest in what they're saying or doing. Once we have a real interest in something, our entire body language changes. Your target will easily detect this and be much more receptive to your ideas, offers or suggestions. Subtle rapport building tricks include mirroring body language or matching the tone and speed of the other person's voice. Matching makes us appear more likable.

➤ Use your words masterfully

Developing good negotiation skills, in business or your private life, is something that can be learned. The first and most simple step is to use words in such a way that makes it easy for others to agree with what you want. For example, instead of asking, 'Would you be able to go on that trip?', say 'How soon can you go?'. This way of asking for someone's compliance implies the outcome has already been agreed. You're effectively not giving them the option to say No. This is also often used in sales negotiations, at the end of a sales pitch the salesperson may ask 'How would you like to pay?', without ever asking for consent if the customer was interested in the product.

➤ Use a Persons' Name or Title repeatedly

In the world-renowned book – How to win friends and influence people, the author Dale Carnegie discovered many factors in becoming more influential. One of the most popular is using someone's name or associated title. He believed that hearing your own name is one of the best and sweetest sounds for each of us. This may go back to our early childhood days when our name was repeated many times in loving tones. A person's name is essentially a core part of who they are, therefore hearing it validates our existence and makes us feel more positive about the person we heard it from. Taking this a step further we can apply titles to people if we want to influence them to behave how we would like, words such as 'mate', 'bro' or 'boss' can help control how other people treat us. Using such terms becomes a self-fulfilling prophecy. The person naturally acts more like what we refer to them as.

This is also seen in the development of young children, sometimes to devastating effect. If a child is constantly being told they're bad or worthless, they'll internalize this belief and grow up believing this to be true resulting in low self-worth.

➤ The Power of Suggestion

This technique is most effective when something unexpected has happened. Or when we feel the proverbial carpet has been pulled out from under our feet. When something happens that throws us off balance, we're much more likely to accept a suggestion that we would normally refuse.

If you choose such an unpredictable moment to suggest a 'solution' to someone's problem, but in fact, you're asking them to do what's in your interests. The other party is much more likely to accept your proposal then they would under normal circumstances. This is because people are more receptive to new ideas when they're disorientated or unsettled. The mind has to work harder to process new or different experiences, which leads to the lowering of other mental functions (such as decision making) for a short period of time.

As a countermeasure, never sign or agree to something when you don't feel fully 'centered' because you are much more vulnerable to manipulation in this state.

Chapter 7: Persuasion

Persuasion is an attempt to convince others to change their behavior. The only problem with conviction is that it is often clear to you that you have to convince someone. They hope you can get the pulse out. There is no point in trying to control a friendly or neutral and destructive party in trying to contain a rival. The trigger is most effective when you can reveal new information and change the minds of others.

If someone changes the program based on the new information you can provide or the new understanding of the information, the trigger has a chance of success. This means providing information that affects the other party's goals or the measures taken to achieve the other party's goals.

The only scenario is when other parties believe that your goals have a positive relationship with your goals. In this case, they trust your judgment and your motivations and will relieve your cause. It's best if you have completely new information or the trust of other stakeholders. But especially not. In such cases, the trigger is only effective when combined with other tools such as fraud. In other words, try to convince someone on the basis of lies or partial truth. Again, you reveal new information or make someone believe that your objectives correspond to theirs, but they create and hide the elements.

Motivation at work (or in another environment) is a way to convince others to follow a course, to recognize an obligation, or to buy a product or service. Employers place special emphasis on employee compliance skills, as they can affect many aspects of the workplace and increase productivity. Stimulation techniques are also used in political and funding campaigns, in public relations, in the legal system, and in other areas. If you want to influence your project participants, you need compliance knowledge. These partners include customers, colleagues, current or potential employers, business partners, subsidiaries, donors, resources, judges, judges, consumers, voters, and potential employees.

Stimulation process

The stimulation process typically includes the following stages:

1. Assess the preferences, needs, and expectations of the target person or group.

It is much easier to convince others and explain how the proposed project is mutually beneficial. In the sales area, this phase of the stimulation process is referred to as "advice." In this phase, a competent sales employee first asks the customer about his preferences and requirements and then offers a product solution.

Example:

Analyze the job and adapt the cover letter to the most important qualifications of the job.

Design an incentive plan for the sales team.

Create a campaign slogan for political candidates.

We sew the copy of the advertisement according to the needs of the target group.

Write a script for a donation over the phone to raise money for a charity.

2. Establish relationships with target groups.

Once you've determined what your target audience needs, you can use this information to build relationships with them. Keep in mind that building trust in many work environments is an endless activity. For example, if you have achieved a group purchase for a project, you must continue to build relationships for future collaboration by praising team members for the good work during the project's final phase.

Example:

Asking customers how their sons and daughters develop at college is part of building relationships with students and their families.

Many thanks to the employees who successfully completed the task.

Write a letter or email to potential donors on behalf of the fundraiser.

One is to praise them after completing the particularly rigorous phases of the training plan.

Recruit volunteers for charitable projects.

3. Formulate the benefits of adopting the proposed agenda or course of action.

In the first phase of enforcement, we created a list of stakeholder needs that we can offer and fully explain the benefits of adopting the plan. In sales, this position is sometimes referred to as a "value-added" suggestion. Regardless of the situation, however, it's a good strategy to focus on the benefits of the product you offer.

Example:

Describe the benefits of working with your employer at a campus recruitment event.

Encourage patients to adopt a healthy lifestyle.

Present the jury's argument during the hearing or hearing process.

Contact management and hire additional staff for your department.

Protect and create a celebrity certificate as part of a product or service promotion.

4. Actively address the concerns of the stakeholders and clarify the objections to the project.

If you need to convince others of the course, it's best to anticipate and prepare for possible objections (someone always tries to throw a wrench at work!). Listening to and respecting others' concerns about new projects and ventures can make it easier to deal with objections.

Example:

Meet with staff to evaluate their response to planned restructuring.

Protect the petition signature.

The management team makes a decision to reduce staff or money.

Explain the need for quality control and deadlines for construction projects.

He leads a recruitment team that evaluates several top candidates in one place.

5. Provide counterpoints for overcoming objections.

This is one of the most difficult stages of the stimulation process. However, if you anticipate potential conflicts, you can convince yourself to collect counterpoints.

Example:

Inform customers more fully about the various benefits of the product or provide a competitive analysis.

Raise pay or negotiate additional leave.

Negotiate or renegotiate the terms of the contract.

An explanation of why senior management increases the department budget.

Dealing with opposing attorneys in litigation.

6. Ensure proper controls for projects.

Disclosure of process transparency and effective challenge for planning is generally open to the persuasion and negotiation of people.

Example:

Accept that the team should work on a smaller budget than you would like.

Accept that if there is a shortage of staff, there will be no additional free time.

Make sure someone had provided you with creative information you didn't know when you first proposed the project.

Understand that you need to increase your pay to attract top employees.

7. Change the plan as needed to find common cause with stakeholders.

Most projects — be it a sales effort or a workplace negotiation — require compromise. It is worthwhile to know in advance what elements of the project can be handled flexibly.

Example:

Conduct union negotiations to raise pay and improve benefits.

Insist on divorce mediators to accept the fair offer.

The company offered a plan to hire an assistant to key vendors. He pointed out that he might leave the company because of workload concerns.

Reduce the fixed price of a product or service.

8. Clarify the terms of the final agreement.

Since shareholders have no clear understanding of the contract or the final terms of the agreement, no one wants to go back and restart the trigger process. Clarity is important when explaining the expected outcome of a contract.

Example:

Inform new employees of employment and / or layoff conditions.

Complete the learning contract with a student in the classroom environment.

Check with the customer before the final identification.

Two weeks ago, we announced that we would be leaving work and the last business day.

9. Follow up to see if shareholders still have questions about the proposal.

Follow-up with stakeholders not only builds relationships but also helps track the success of the approved company.

Example:

Design and distribute customer opinion polls.

Review of online product reviews after product launch.

Call the patient after a medical or dental procedure to check for healing.

Before the project is officially released, ask the client if the final changes are necessary.

Is trust a skill you can learn?

Beliefs such as confidence and charisma are "soft skills" for many. This is often an inherent personality trait.

Chapter 8: Using Dark Psychology To Manage Emotions

Negative Emotions and How to Control Them

What are Negative Emotions?

It's essential to recognize what a feeling is and what an inclination is. While the two are interconnected, there's a greater distinction than you may understand. It's unquestionably something that shocked me when I started with my examination.

Feelings – Emotions are viewed as 'lower level' reactions. They initially happen in the subcortical regions of the mind, for example, the amygdala and the ventromedial prefrontal cortices. These territories are answerable for delivering biochemical responses that directly affect your physical state.

Feelings are coded into our DNA and are thought to have created as an approach to assist us with reacting rapidly to various ecological dangers, much like our 'battle or flight' reaction. The amygdala has additionally been appeared to assume a job in the arrival of synapses that are basic for memory, which is the reason enthusiastic recollections are frequently more grounded and simpler to review.

Feelings have a more grounded physical establishing than sentiments meaning specialists discover them simpler to gauge equitably through physical prompts, for example, blood stream, pulse, mind movement, outward appearances, and non-verbal communication.

Sentiments – Emotions are viewed as going before emotions, which will in general be our responses to the various feelings we experience. Where feelings can have an increasingly summed up understanding over all people, sentiments are progressively emotional and are impacted by our own encounters and elucidations of our reality dependent on those encounters.

Sentiments happen in the neocortical districts of the cerebrum and are the following stage by they way we react to our feelings as a person. Since they are so abstract, they can't be estimated the manner in which feelings can.

Clinicians have since quite a while ago investigated the scope of human feelings and their definitions. Eckman (1999) recognized six beginning essential feelings:

- Anger

- Disgust

- Fear

- Happiness

- Sadness

- Surprise

Later developed this to incorporate a further eleven fundamental feelings:

- Amusement

- Contempt

- Contentment

- Embarrassment

- Excitement

- Guilt

- Pride

- Relief

- Satisfaction

- Sensory Pleasure

- Shame

Contrary feelings "as a terrible or despondent feeling which is evoked in people to express an antagonistic impact towards an occasion or individual." Reading through the rundown of Eckman's essential feelings, it's very simple to decide those that may be alluded to as 'adverse' feelings.

While we can utilize the name negative, with what we think about feelings, recognize that all feelings are totally typical to encounter. They are a piece of our instilled DNA. What is increasingly significant, is getting when and why negative feelings may emerge, and creating positive practices to address them.

A Look at the Psychology of Emotions

One of the more famous mental speculations of feelings is Robert Plutchik's Wheel of Emotions. Plutchik (1980) expressed that there are eight essential feelings: bliss, trust, dread, shock, misery, expectation, outrage and appall. Plutchik went further by blending the feelings with their contrary energies and afterward making the wheel of feelings, which serves to expound on how intricate and intuitive our feelings are.

Plutchik's wheel is a solid visual portrayal of how our feelings present themselves. As should be obvious the center feeling diminishes as you move outward on the wheel. Plutchik likewise utilized shading to speak to the power of the feeling: the darker the shading, the more extraordinary it is. So at its most extraordinary trust becomes deference, and at any rate exceptional, acknowledgment.

It's a fabulous beginning asset for helping us further build up our comprehension of how our feelings present themselves, how they vacillate and how they can cooperate with one another. It has educated further mental research around there and is regularly the establishment from which specialists investigating feelings have based their examination.

A 'tree' of feelings which broke feelings into essential, optional and tertiary measurements. This incorporates 6 essential feelings (love, euphoria, shock, outrage, pity, and dread), with related feelings that create at the auxiliary level, and again at the tertiary level. For instance, if the essential feeling is happiness, the auxiliary feelings could incorporate gladness, positive thinking or enthrallment and the tertiary level could incorporate delight, triumph or expectation.

Another level and built up 'The Hourglass of Emotions'. In their book, they based on Plutchik's eight essential feelings and separated them into four measurements: affectability, consideration, loveliness, and fitness. They likewise made qualifications between which of the feelings were sure (satisfaction, trust, outrage, and expectation) or negative (nauseate, pity, dread, and shock).

8 Examples of Negative Emotions

As we've investigated, negative feelings are totally typical. Without them, we wouldn't have the option to acknowledge positive ones. Simultaneously, on and when you discover you reliably have an inclination towards one specific feeling — particularly a negative one — it merits investigating why that may be.

8 of the more typical negative feelings and why they may emerge:

Anger

Ever have somebody let you know no to accomplish something you need? How does that make you feel? Does your blood start to heat up, your temperature rise and do you figuratively 'see red'? This is regularly how outrage is portrayed. Your body is responding to things not going your direction, and it's an endeavor to attempt to amend that.

Regularly when we're irate we'll yell, our face will enlist our resentment and we may even toss things around. We're attempting to get our own specific manner in a circumstance and this is the main way we can think how. In case you're frequently responding to situations along these lines, it's a smart thought to investigate why and think of progressively positive methodologies.

Annoyance

Do you have a partner who maybe talks too noisily? Does your accomplice consistently leave their filthy dishes in the sink? Despite the fact that we may like our associate and love our accomplice these practices can make us feel truly irritated. Alluding to Pluchik's wheel, you can see that inconvenience is the more fragile type of outrage. While not as extraordinary as outrage, it's the aftereffect of a comparable perspective — something has occurred or somebody is accomplishing something you wish they wouldn't. What's more, you have no influence over it.

Fear

Dread is frequently refered to as one of the center fundamental feelings, and that is on the grounds that it's intensely connected with our feeling of self-protection. It's a developed reaction to caution us about hazardous circumstances, sudden deterrents or disappointments. We don't feel dread so as to feel troubled, despite what might be expected, it's there to assist us with exploring potential risk effectively. Grasping the feeling of dread and investigating why it emerges can assist you with setting yourself up proactively to handle difficulties.

Anxiety

Much like dread, tension looks to caution us about potential dangers and threats. It's frequently observed as a negative feeling as it's idea having an on edge demeanor impedes judgment and our capacity to act. New look into has discovered the inverse.

Having tension elevated members capacity to perceive faces with furious or dreadful demeanors. They estimated electrical flag in the cerebrum and found that non-clinically analyzed members moved their vitality from tactile (communicating the feeling) to engine (physical activity) circuits. Essentially, members with uneasiness were progressively prepared to react and respond to apparent dangers.

Sadness

At the point when you miss a cutoff time, get an awful evaluation, or don't verify that activity you had your expectations stuck on, you'll likely feel pitiful. Misery happens when we are disappointed with ourselves, our accomplishments or the conduct of another person around us. Bitterness can be great to encounter as it shows to us that we energetic about something. It very well may be an incredible impetus to seek after change.

Guilt

Blame is a mind boggling feeling. We can feel this in connection to ourselves and past practices that we wish hadn't occurred, yet in addition in connection to how our conduct impacts people around us. Blame is regularly alluded to as an 'ethical feeling' and can be another solid impetus to urge us to make changes throughout our life.

Apathy

Like blame, aloofness can be a perplexing feeling. In the event that you've lost energy, inspiration or enthusiasm for the things you've recently appreciated, this could be identified with lack of care. Like outrage, it can emerge when we lose power over a situation or circumstance yet as opposed to losing control, we seek after a progressively aloof forceful articulation of insubordination.

Despair

Ever attempted to accomplish a specific undertaking or objective on numerous occasions and not succeeded? Did that make you want to toss your hands noticeable all around, and outdoors in bed with an enormous tub of frozen yogurt for organization? That is sadness and it's a feeling that emerges when we aren't getting the outcomes we need. Despondency gives us a reason to abandon our ideal objectives and it returns to a self-safeguarding strategy. Gloom can really be a valuable suggestion to take a break and reestablish, before proceeding to seek after a difficult objective.

What Causes Negative Emotions and Why Do We Have Them?

When you start investigating negative feelings somewhat more, you can truly begin to perceive what may cause or trigger them, and why we have them in any case.

As far as causes, it could be various things for instance:

- Anxiety looked about going to a meeting for a new position

- Anger at being up to speed in rush hour gridlock

- Sadness at encountering a separation

- Annoyance that a partner hasn't taken the necessary steps for a major venture

- Despair at not having the option to adhere to another exercise system

Feelings are a wellspring of data that help you comprehend what is happening around you. Negative feelings, specifically, can assist you with perceiving dangers and feel arranged to decidedly deal with potential threats.

Various encounters in our lives will induce distinctive passionate responses, to varying degrees of power. As a person, you will encounter a full scope of feelings all through your lifetime in light of quickly evolving circumstances.

Would We Like to Overcome and Stop Negative Emotions Altogether?

It's typical for us to need to move away from feelings that make us feel awful. As a transformative reaction, negative feelings in the cutting edge world are not so much a sign of a serious danger against us, however surviving and halting them by and large would be tremendously unfavorable to us.

Negative feelings are an extraordinarily typical, sound and accommodating piece of life. I believe it's extremely significant not to fall into the 'bliss trap' of accepting that these feelings are an indication of shortcoming or low passionate knowledge. I know from individual experience that attempting to conceal away from negative feelings, can prompt further passionate torment.

As a person, you will encounter a full scope of feelings all through your lifetime in light of quickly evolving circumstances. No feeling is without reason. It's the point at which we start to additionally investigate and comprehend the reason behind every feeling, that we adapt better approaches to react which underpins our enthusiastic development and feeling of prosperity.

When investigating negative feelings, it's likewise essential to realize that they are by all account not the only wellspring of data you approach. Before you follow up on any feeling you ought to likewise look to investigate your past encounters, put away information and recollections, individual qualities and wanted results for some random situation. Keep in mind – feelings are a low-level response so you get the chance to choose how you react to them and not let them commandeer your conduct.

What are the Effects of Negative Emotions?

While understanding that negative feelings are a solid piece of life is significant, there is a drawback to giving them an excess of free rule.

On and when you invest a lot of energy harping on negative feelings and the circumstances that may have caused them, you could go into a winding of rumination. Rumination is the propensity to continue thinking, replaying, or fixating on negative passionate circumstances and encounters. In this winding of negative reasoning, you can wind up feeling more regrettable and more awful about the circumstance and yourself, the consequence of which could be various inconvenient impacts to your psychological and physical prosperity.

The issue with rumination is that it builds your cerebrum's pressure reaction circuit, which means your body gets pointlessly overwhelmed with the pressure hormone cortisol. There's extensive proof this is a driver for clinical sorrow.

Further examine has connected the propensity to ruminate to various hurtful adapting practices, for example, indulging, smoking and liquor utilization, nearby physical wellbeing results including a sleeping disorder, hypertension, cardiovascular malady, and clinical nervousness and despondency.

Another study found that individuals who enjoyed delayed rumination after a negative enthusiastic encounter took more time to recuperate from the physiological effect of the experience.

Rumination can be a troublesome escape clause to escape, particularly as the vast majority don't understand they're stuck in ruminating trench and rather accept they are effectively critical thinking. This can prompt further ramifications for mental and physical prosperity.

5 Proven Benefits of Negative Emotions

It's not all fate and anguish. At the point when dealt with well, negative feelings can have demonstrated advantages for our prosperity, and undeniably more research has been filled investigating this part of negative feelings.

1. Misery can assist you with giving more consideration to detail

Where positive feelings signal that everything is great in our prompt condition, negative feelings alert us that there are difficulties or new improvements that requires our increasingly engaged consideration. Bitterness sends us the ready that something isn't right and asks us to direct our concentration toward for what reason this might be, what may be causing it, and what we have to do to fix it.

2. Outrage can be a solid spark to look for intercession

Outrage is just trailed by animosity in around 10% of situations. Outrage has been demonstrated to urge you to search out dynamic practices to address situations or individuals you've discovered hazardous however doesn't really mean through showdown or physical acts. Outrage is a solid ready that urges you to consider why somebody may be carrying on a specific way, and what you can do to reestablish harmony.

3. Tension energizes better approaches for moving toward issues and difficulties

At the point when we feel on edge, we'll attempt to do anything we can not to feel that way any longer. Nervousness is firmly connected to our 'battle or flight' reaction, which enables your body to make vitality rapidly, good to go. At the point when looked with risky circumstances, uneasiness will dominate and urge us to look for arrangements rapidly so as to escape peril.

4. Blame causes you change negative conduct

Blame can be a particularly valuable feeling. It's basically our ethical compass and when it goes off, it's a decent sign that we may have carried on or said something frightful to somebody we care about. It resembles our inside framework for rebuffing ourselves when we've accomplished something incorrectly.

Individuals who are increasingly inclined to feeling remorseful are more averse to take, take drugs, resort to viciousness or drink and drive.

5. Desire persuades you to work more earnestly

Desire isn't constantly vindictive. More often than not it's what analysts allude to as 'amiable envy'. Generous envy has been appeared to urge understudies to perform better on tests and in homework, as observing another understudy accomplish a decent evaluation made it increasingly substantial for them to accomplish as well. Next time you feel envious in light of the fact that another person has accomplished an ideal objective, attempt to consider this to be something worth being thankful for — it implies the objective is absolutely feasible for you as well.

How Might We Best Control and Deal with our Negative Emotions?

Probably the most ideal approaches to manage our negative feelings is through acknowledgment. Similarly as there are advantages to negative feelings, driving ourselves to be cheerful all the time can likewise be adverse to our general passionate prosperity.

Tolerating negative feelings, in ourselves as well as other people, are each of the a piece of being human enables us to manufacture better empathy for how they may introduce themselves and why. As opposed to getting stuck in an outlook that negative feelings should be kept away from or that they are by one way or another 'wrong' to encounter, we have to acknowledge they are a characteristic piece of what our identity is.

When we do that we can truly start to change how we may react to them and create practices that are important and carry an incentive to how we convey what needs be and draw in with others.

6 Tips to Manage, Process and Embrace Negative Emotions

As positive brain science has increased more understanding into our negative feelings, it's additionally had the option to furnish us with various methodologies for adjusting these feelings inside our everyday lives.

Approaches to proactively process and recognize negative feelings and thought of the abbreviation tears of would like to help mentor and guide people. This is what it represents:

T = Teach and Learn

This is the way toward tuning in to what your body is attempting to show you through the introduction of negative feelings, and realize what they mean. It's structure your very own insight into the manner in which you react to enthusiastic states, translating the sign your body is sending you, and recognizing that they fill a need.

E = Express and empower

Negative feelings urge us to express them. They are truly significant feelings. The express and empower some portion of the abbreviation urges you to investigate this with transparency and interest. It's tied in with expanding your acknowledgment of your normal senses and empowering them to be available without hatred.

A= Accept and get to know

This pursues on pleasantly from express and empower. It's tied in with get to know yourself and the manner in which you are as a human. Concentrate on expanding your acknowledgment with positive certifications to bring your circle of negative feelings into a space of acknowledgment.

R = Re-assess and re-outline

When you've started to acknowledge this is a characteristic piece of what your identity is, you can start to concentrate on reframing the circumstance and how you respond. Because a negative feeling has emerged, doesn't mean you need to respond in manners that are hindering to you and people around you.

Tolerating negative feelings isn't tied in with tolerating or pardoning poor practices, it's tied in with making mindfulness for oneself as well as other people to make constructive responses.

S = Social help

Realizing that negative feelings are available within each one of us, and in essentially a similar way, can be a phenomenal wellspring of sympathy and compassion to people around us. It's the manner by which we process our feelings that contrast, so observing somebody in the tosses of outrage, realizing that they are simply taking care of an apparent risk can truly urge us to move toward them with sympathy, instead of outrage ourselves.

H = Hedonic prosperity and joy

This is the way toward gathering positive encounters with negative. Since we all the more promptly review negative encounters, it very well may be helpful for us to gather them with positive encounters so we don't fall into a ruminating trap. Along these lines, we can concentrate a greater amount of our vitality on reviewing the positive encounters.

O = Observe and visit

Set aside the effort to truly watch your responses without disregarding them, quelling them, or over overstating them. Use care to carry your concentration to your mind and body and what a specific feeling is making inside you. Take care of these responses without judgment.

P = Physiology and conduct changes

Similarly as you watch your enthusiastic and mental reactions, watch your physiological responses as well. Carry your concentration to your breath, your pulse and sense out the adjustments in your physiology that a negative feeling may have caused. Once more, take care of these progressions without judgment.

E = Eudaimonia

This probably won't be a word you know about, yet it's well worth adding to your jargon. Eudaimonia is a Greek word which fundamentally alludes to having a decent soul. It implies you have discovered a condition of being that is cheerful, sound and prosperous, and you have figured out how to take part in activities that outcome in your general prosperity. It implies you're effectively endeavoring towards a feeling of realness in everything you do.

Beneath tips to enable you to oversee, process and grasp negative feelings in manners that will assist you with understanding and discover an incentive in them:

Envisage your 'Most ideal Self'

In the event that you have a feeling that your negative feelings are defeating you, that you're not communicating them in solid manners or stalling out in ruminating practices, a straightforward perception strategy could help.

Rather than concentrating just on the negative feeling or what you're fouling up, center rather around what you might want the conduct to be.

What does the most ideal adaptation of you look like in that situation? How might they respond? What might they say? How might they feel? What might they do after? You can do this as a psychological visual exercise or a diary work out.

Taking the time once per week to rehearse this can have astounding results on your state of mind as well as how you approach the situation next opportunity it comes around.

Practice Gratitude

Rehearsing appreciation has been appeared to have superb impacts for both the beneficiaries and providers. These impacts have long arriving at impacts on our temperament and impression of occasions, so it merits investing a smidgen of energy adding the training to your week after week collection.

Regardless of whether it's for a little thing or a major thing, face to face, via telephone, a letter or a straightforward instant message, telling somebody you value them or something they have done, can truly have any kind of effect by they way you see and react to negative feelings.

Explore care systems

On and when you discover you have a short breaker and outrage is your go-to negative feeling (or on and when you find you're generally on the range of the displeasure feeling, routinely encountering irritation) care could help to reframe what you're feeling.

Pursue the tears of expectation direction and set aside the effort to comprehend why you might be reacting along these lines. Care can assist you with finding the headspace to do this in a positive way.

Learn how to react versus respond

Do you know the distinction between how you react versus how you respond? Negative feelings frequently urge us to respond promptly to a given situation. At the point when we feel furious, we may lash out or yell. At the point when we become miserable, we may pull back and dismiss individuals around us.

Now and again we have to follow up on these driving forces, yet for the most part we don't. By investigating your negative feelings you can begin to build up your comprehension of how you respond, and rather begin to change this to positive methods for reacting – which could mean discovering that no response is required by any stretch of the imagination.

Know when to take a break

Realize when to take a day to yourself. In the event that you are always encountering negative feelings and attempting to oversee them, your body is revealing to you something isn't right.

Take a day to re-focus. Fill this day with positive encounters, accomplishing the things that you know fuel you and make you feel better. This sort of break can realign your reasoning, give you some space to refocus on why you may be encountering the negative feelings, and think of some positive adapting systems.

8 Tips to Change Negative Thinking

Negative thinking adds to tension in social and execution circumstances. Most treatments for social uneasiness include an angle devoted to changing negative speculation styles into progressively accommodating and positive methods for taking a gander at circumstances.

The way to changing your negative musings is to see how you think now (and the issues that outcome) and afterward use systems to change considerations or make them have less impact. For the most part, these means are completed with an advisor, however they can likewise be utilized as a component of a self improvement exertion toward defeating social tension. The following are eight articles to assist you with changing your negative idea designs.

Understand Your Thinking Styles

One of the initial moves toward changing your negative reasoning examples is seeing precisely how you think at the present time. Here is a rundown of 10 kinds of "flawed" thinking designs that may be pushing you into difficulty.

For instance, on and when you will in general view yourself as a total achievement or disappointment in each circumstance, at that point you are taking part in "highly contrasting" thinking. These 10 reasoning examples vary in unobtrusive manners yet they all include bends of the real world and nonsensical methods for taking a gander at circumstances and individuals.

How to Stop Thinking Negatively

One of the fundamental parts of a treatment plan including intellectual conduct treatment (CBT) is subjective rebuilding. This procedure encourages you to distinguish and change your negative musings into increasingly supportive and versatile reactions.

Regardless of whether done in treatment or all alone, subjective rebuilding includes a bit by bit process whereby negative contemplations are distinguished, assessed for exactness, and afterward supplanted.

Despite the fact that from the outset, it is hard to think with this new style, after some time and with training, positive and balanced considerations will come all the more normally.

How to Cope With Criticism

Notwithstanding intellectual rebuilding, another part of CBT that is now and then supportive includes something known as the "confident guard of oneself." Since it is conceivable that a portion of the time, individuals will really be basic and critical, it is significant that you can adapt to dismissal.

This procedure is typically directed in treatment with an imagine discussion among you and your advisor to develop your confidence abilities and self-assured reactions to analysis. These abilities are then moved to this present reality through schoolwork assignments.

How to Practice Mindfulness

Care has its underlying foundations in reflection. It is simply the act of segregating from your contemplations and feelings and review them as an outside spectator.

During care preparing, you will figure out how to see your musings and emotions as articles gliding past you that you can stop and watch or let cruise you by.

The goal of care is to deal with your enthusiastic responses to circumstances by permitting the thinking part about your cerebrum to dominate.

Why Thought Stopping Doesn't Work

Thought halting is something contrary to care. It is the demonstration of being vigilant for negative musings and demanding that they are disposed of.

The issue with thought halting is that the more you attempt to stop your negative contemplations the more they will surface. Care is desirable over idea halting on the grounds that it gives less weight to your musings and diminishes the effect they have on you.

Figured halting may appear to help temporarily, yet in the long haul, it prompts more tension.

Understanding Thought Diaries

Thought journals are instruments that can be utilized as a feature of any procedure to change negative reasoning. Thought journals help you to recognize your negative reasoning styles and addition a superior comprehension of how your contemplations (and not the circumstances you are in) cause your enthusiastic responses.

Most intellectual conduct treatment plans will include the utilization of an idea journal that you will finish as a feature of day by day schoolwork assignments.

Sample Thought Diary

Not certain what a real idea journal resembles? Here is an example structure that you can use to record your considerations and inspect the association between your negative reasoning styles and your enthusiastic responses.

How to Complete a Thought Diary

Here is a bit by bit portrayal of how to round out an idea journal like the example structure above.

In this specific model, we separate the perspective of an individual out on the town, and the enthusiastic and physical responses that outcome from negative reasoning examples.

Before the finish of the idea investigation, we have supplanted silly musings about dismissal with progressively supportive and positive perspectives.

Chapter 9: What Machiavellianism Is

Machiavellianism in psychology describes a personality trait which sees an individual so concentrated on their own interests they will control, deceive, and exploit others to attain their objectives.

Machiavellianism is just one of the qualities in what's called the 'Dark Triad', the other 2 being narcissism and psychopathy.

The term itself stems from a referral to the infamous Niccolò Machiavelli, a diplomat and theorist in the Renaissance whose most widely known work ended up being 'The Prince" (Il Principe). This well-known book upheld his views that strong rulers should be harsh with their subjects and nemeses, and that glory and survival justified any means, even ones that were considered unethical and brutal.

By the late 16th century "Machiavellianism" became a well-known word to specify the art of being deceptive to get ahead.

Just find a therapist

But it wasn't a mental term until the 1970s, when 2 social psychologists, Richard Christie and Florence L. Geis, developed what they called "the Machiavellianism Scale". A character stock that is still used as the primary assessment tool for Machaivellianism, this scale is now called 'the Mach-IV test".

Machiavellianism has been found to be more common in men then women. It can, though, occur in anybody-- even kids.

Signs of Machiavellianism

Machiavellianism in psychology. Someone with the trait of Machiavellianism will tend to have many of the following propensities:

only concentrated on their own ambition and interests

focus on money and power over relationships

encountered as charming and positive

make use of and control others to get ahead

lie and deceive when required

using flattery a lot

not having in principles and values

can come across as aloof or hard to actually learn more about

negative of goodness and morality

efficient in triggering others hurt to achieve their means

low levels of empathy

often stay away from commitment and emotional attachments

can be very patient due to computing nature

rarely reveal their true intentions

susceptible to one-night stand encounters

can be good at reading social situations and others

lack of warmth in social interactions

not always knowledgeable about the effects of their actions

may have a hard time to determine their own emotions

The Machiavellianism Scale

The Machiavellianism scale is a rating of up to 100 arising from a test that consists of a series of questions. People who score above 60 are considered 'high Machs' and those scoring below 60, 'low Machs'.

High Machs are concentrated on their own wellness. They actually believe that to get ahead, one must be deceptive. They do not rely on human goodness and think depending upon others is naive. Prioritizing power over love and connection, they do not actually believe that mankind is by nature good.

A low Mach, on the other hand, tends to show empathy to others, and is sincere and trusting. They believe in human goodness and that if you abide by good morals you're going to succeed in life. Too short on the scale, however, can see people being submissive and too acceptable.

There is also a 'Kiddie Mach Test' for children.

Associated mental conditions to Machiavellianism

Machiavellianism is considered part of the 'Dark Triad', being one of three personality traits that also includes narcissism and sociopathy/ psychopathy. With every of these traits alone making someone hard to be around, all 3 taking place in a single person can produce somebody that is rather hazardous to other people's psychological wellbeing.

Despite relatively clear connections between the 3 'dark triad' qualities and the frequency of one quality usually occurring with the other 2, research has yet to be done to concretely prove a correlation.

Personality conditions where sufferers might have the trait of Machiavellianism include Antisocial personality disorder, and Narcissistic personality disorder.

A current research study also found a high occurrence of sadness in those with the Machiavellian trait.

What is the difference between the three characteristics of the dark triad?

All 3 characteristics are about attempting to get away with putting yourself initially to get what you really want. But they each have a very different focus.

Machiavellianism is mostly about manipulation for personal gain.

Narcissism is mostly about believing you deserve adoration and to be treated differently than others.

Sociopathy is mainly about being cold and insensitive to others' needs.

How is Machiavellianism treated?

The issue with malicious personality traits like those found in the dark triad is that the ones that have such traits are unlikely to seek therapy or want to change. They normally only attend treatment if pushed to do so by relatives or because they have committed a criminal offense and have been told to attend therapy by court order.

For psychiatric therapy to be efficient, a client needs to be truthful and allow a trusting relationship to form between themselves and their therapist. Machiavellianism is a quality whereby a person is often dishonest and doesn't trust others.

And yet with a well-informed psychotherapist development can be made. A great psychotherapist with experience of the qualities of the Dark Triad will see each customer as an individual and consider their special history. This will consist of the conditioning they have experienced and their unique life situation. An experienced therapist can also determine and help deal with other related concerns the person has, like depression and anxiety.

Cognitive behavior therapy is one type of treatment that's at times advised for those with sinister personality traits. It embraces that the way we think dictates our conduct, so by identifying and changing disordered ideas and feelings we can then transform behavior.

How Do I Know If I Have the Machiavellian Characteristic?

While you can find your rating on the Machiavellian Scale by trying the test online, self analysis isn't advised. If you truly are worried you have the quality a proper diagnosis with a mental health specialist is suggested.

I Am Sure My Boss/ Ex/ Family Member Has the Machiavellianism Trait, So What Do I Do?

The problem then lies in the simple fact that those who do have the Machiavellian quality rarely will want to change or look for help.

Obviously, it's also easy to assume others have the traits of the 'dark triad' like Machiavellianism, and while tons of do, it is best not to leap to conclusions.

If, however, you feel you are the victim of someone with the Machiavellian characteristic, what you CAN do is seek help and support for yourself.

It can be frustrating and trigger great psychological distress and damage to have such an individual in your life, and their capability to control may leave you doubting your own instincts or feeling co-dependently 'addicted' to having them in your life. A therapist can help you learn better self-care, and help you set boundaries or if possible, extricate the person from your life for good.

Chapter 10: Deception- Beyond The Little White Lie

Everyone's done it. Small children don't know who made the mess or broke the lamp. The check is in the mail. We'll be ready in five minutes. Yes, you look wonderful in that dress. The little white lie. It's inherent in human nature. Before we look at how we can use lies and deception, let's look at why we lie.

Lies!

If humans are hardwired to lie, why? Where does the instinct to tell an untruth come from? Is it biological or psychological, or both? The answer is both! Humans lie because of what scientists call a 'tend and defend' response. This means that lies are used to tend to needs or to defend against the threat, and there is a correlation between lying and the release of the brain chemical oxytocin, one of our innate 'feel good' hormones. When we have elevated levels of oxytocin, we are more likely to lie to avoid losing that feeling of a natural high.

There are several documented reasons for lying, which fall into either the tend or defend category. They are as follows:

1- Defend oneself- these are lies made to avoid punishment or backlash for action or perceived action;

2- Defend others- these are lies made to avoid others being punished or attacked for their actions or perceived actions;

3- Tend to oneself- these are lies told to gain control of a situation or a person, lies told to avoid embarrassment or awkward social situations, or lies told to gain personal desires or win admiration; and

4- Tend to others- lies told to protect others' secrets, to build other people up into greater figures than they are, and to maintain social facades.

Lies don't have to be earth-shattering, but when they become too big, it often becomes extremely difficult to keep a story straight. They say the best lies have an element of truth, and that seems to be the case. Lies often have harsh consequences when they are discovered, so if you are going to be deceptive, be sure to be emotionally prepared to deal with any fallout.

The fallout from Pinocchio's lies manifested physically as a growing nose!

When Do Lies Become Deception?

If you stop to think about lies, you'll realize that they almost have a scale. A little white lie about not having a babysitter might get you out of going to a party, so that's pretty low on the scale. But if you lie about not having a babysitter, but you don't need one because you are lying about having a baby, now that's a bit of a whopper. So where is the line?

Small lies, or fibs, often don't have many consequences. But larger lies, especially those that become compounded by repetition or addition, lead to a cycle of lying that eventually becomes destructive to self, others, or self. That cycle is most likely the definitive line between a lie and a deception.

Deception comes in many forms- lying about work or life experience, lying about the state of your relationships, lies of omission, and even lies which are told so many times, the liar themselves believe them. If lies can cause so much psychological damage, why do people still insist on using them?

How Lies Apply in Real Life

It goes back to that 'tend or defend' response. Let's take a more in-depth look at why people could use lies for those purposes. The first reason on the list was to 'defend oneself'. Self-preservation is a powerful thing. If you are in an abusive relationship, you might lie about where you've been to avoid being verbally or physically attacked, even if your location would be somewhere perfectly harmless in a healthy relationship. If your abuser thinks you were at the grocery store rather than having coffee with a friend, you've lied to protect yourself from abuse.

The second reason was to defend others. This may follow closely a scenario like above, but perhaps it's a mother lying to protect her children from a physically or emotionally abusive authority figure.

Another scenario might be an older sibling taking the blame for misbehaving when it was really the younger sibling that caused a mess or broke something valuable. Friends or coworkers may lie to stick up for each other in situations that they might otherwise get in trouble for.

The next item on the list about why people lie is to tend to themselves. There are many selfish reasons to lie, and it's probably the most common reason as well. People lie to take care of their own needs and desires, in order to get what they want from others. People lie because they want other people to like them, and so they exaggerate personal accomplishments and achievements to make themselves look better. We hear of this in cases of a transcript or resume fraud.

Lies that people tell to tend to themselves also frequently are told, no maliciously, but with the intent of covering up an embarrassing situation or avoid an awkward social interaction. These lies might be to hide a slip-up or to skip a party you don't want to attend. While these are little white lies, you may still face a little backlash when your husband's annoying cousin finds out you weren't really too ill to attend her bridal shower two hours away.

The last category of lie is the one that people tell to tend to others. This can mean being deceptive about liking someone's new haircut or lying about how good someone is at their job to help them get a good reference. Lies that we tell to tend to others tend to be lies of a positive nature, but that doesn't mean that they won't be susceptible to the same negative impacts as the other types of lies.

Famous Instances of Deception

Deception is one of the most ubiquitous methods are dark psychology. We see deception used in almost every era of human history. The Trojan Horse is a fabulous example of the power of trickery and deceit. A whole population believed they were receiving a gift, and instead, ended up with a massacre.

In the modern age, one of the largest stories to come out of a basis of deception is the rise and fall of Elizabeth Holmes and her health technology business Theranos. Holmes claimed to have invented a blood testing machine which could run full diagnoses with a minute amount of blood, primarily through a finger-stick. Holmes had her investors and board of directors completely fooled, and these weren't some joes off the street.

Billionaire media mogul Rupert Murdoch, the Walton family of Walmart fame, and the DeVos family, founders of Amway, all fell prey to Holmes's deceptions as investors in her biotech firm. She even fooled many well-heeled and well-educated board members, including several former or future United States Presidential Cabinet members. Holmes's house of cards came tumbling down when it was revealed that her miraculous blood testing equipment was deeply flawed and may have even risked the health of the people who'd relied on it. Prior to her lies being discovered, Holmes had managed to accumulate a net worth of $4.5 billion, all of which is gone today.

Holmes somehow hoodwinked some of the biggest scientific and entrepreneurial names in the country and in the world. Now that's some serious deception!

The Art of Crafting a Good Lie

Telling a lie and selling a lie are two completely different things. Everyone knows when a preschooler is lying about who painted the living room wall. But when it's time to practice deception, how do you put together a story that's believable and watertight?

To tell an effective lie, it must be in part based in truth. It will be easier to remember, and you'll have a defense that you only bent the truth, not outright lied, should you get caught. You also should make your lie as simple as possible, to have fewer details to potentially mess up. If you have time to create your deception, practice telling it. It will come out much more naturally when it's time to tell it.

You shouldn't try to include anyone else in your lies-the more people who know what's happening, the greater chance of you getting caught. Lies and secrets are best kept to yourself. You should keep things brief and talk in your normal tone of voice when you deliver your lie. Make sure your body language and eye contact match your words and be sure that you could convince yourself of what you're trying to say.

Once you've told your lie, destroy any evidence. If you made a social media post, delete it. If you wrote something down, make sure you get rid of the piece of paper. Most importantly, don't compound your lie with another lie. If you get caught, it's probably best just to confess. Why? Because if you come clean and are honest, you're less likely to get caught the next time.

Pants on Fire

Wouldn't it be wonderful if you could actually catch someone in a lie because their pants went up in flames? Unfortunately, liar, liar, pants on fire isn't a real phenomenon. There are ways to tell if someone is lying, no flames involved. Watch someone's eyes when they speak to you; if they seem unable to make eye contact or are very fidgety, they may not be being truthful with you.

Being able to spot a lie goes beyond fidgeting and shifty eyes, though. If someone has a delay in speech or a behavioral pause that they don't normally exhibit, they may be lying to you. Some experts say that a tell-tale sign of lying is if someone who doesn't normally touch their face or throat does so while speaking; likewise for playing with or running their fingers through their hair.

Speech signals could also denote when someone is lying to you. If someone repeats very simple questions before answering you, they could be buying time to craft a false response. You should also take note of any vagueness or lack of details when asked a direct question. If you suspect you're being lied to, ask the person to tell you their story again, but in reverse. The cognitive power it takes to remember a lie may make them slip up if they need to tell it out of order.

While there is no foolproof way to determine if someone is lying to you, use these tips and go with your gut, and you'll find that you'll improve your chances of ratting out a liar. Don't discount your instincts, they can tell you more than body language or speech patterns ever will.

Chapter 11: Undetected Mind Control

Mind control has been termed as a form of manipulation, brainwashing, coercive persuasion, thought reform, mental control, and coercive control, among other terms. However, despite the many names used to explain what mind control is, it has a simple universally acceptable definition.

Mind control can be defined as a system of influences that majorly disrupt a person at their core, their preferences, belief, behaviors, values, relationships, and decisions and create a new pseudo-identity or persona. Though the name mind control comes out as a bad thing, if used well, it is useful in some cases like helping addicts transform.

However, in dark psychology, mind control is used unethically. It is a process by which personal or collective freedoms or action is compromised by agents or persons that distort or modify perception, cognition, motivation, behavioral outcomes or affect. This is a form of manipulation to deny personal freedom of choice and thoughts. Mind control is what results in the formation of cults and sects. People lose the ability to think or reason for themselves instead they follow everything their cult leader says.

Who Uses Mind Control?

You may be curious to know who would use these techniques to destroy others for their own gain. or manipulate others because they can and want to control others. The answer is sociopaths or psychopaths and narcissists. The only explanation as to why they do it is simply lack of conscience.

When people do not know about these scholarly names, they call the manipulators abusive or controlling wife or husband, jealous boyfriend, strict boss, or verbally abusive woman among other names. When closely scrutinized, it is found that these people suffer from various personality disorders.

Undetected Mind Control Tactics

Various tactics are used by people every day to control others for their selfish gains. Difficult people that want to control others are everywhere. From the workplace, intimate relationships or friendships, mind control is rampant. It is important to be cognizant of these control tactics so that you can stay away from them.

Below, we shall discuss a few controlling tactics that manipulators often use to maneuver others to be disadvantaged and for them to have an upper hand over them. However, it is important to also know that not everyone that uses these tactics wants to control you. Some people just don't know how to behave and if told, they are likely to stop. Some of these control tactics include:

Time dominance and home-court advantage

A controlling and aggressive person may insist on having a meeting and interacting with you at a location that is advantageous to them. He wants to be in a space where he can exercise his dominance and control to get what he wants.

Apart from location, a controlling person will want to control how long a meeting takes to their advantage. They may want to make it very long to tire you or short to cut you off abruptly before you can express your opinion.

Causing you to wait

If you had an appointment with a person at a particular time, you get there on time, but the person deliberately makes you wait, he or she is simply exercising their power over you. This is a classic form of power play and the message is that their time is more important than yours and that he or she is also more important than you. They want to make you feel that you need them and they don't need you, so you must be the one patient with them.

Furniture set-up to insinuate differences in power

This mostly happens in office setups where you find a person has set up their office in such a way to exercise power. They make sure their seat is large and adjustable indicating executive while you are given a small chair. When seated, they look like they are over you and you are below them. He or she also dominates the tablespace making sure her things have fully occupied the desk and you have no space to place even a laptop. In some cases, the table is used as a sign of emotional, physical barrier or creating a psychological distance.

Calling your name deliberately

Someone can call your name strategically or deliberately as a form of power play. When a person calls out the name of another person, they have their attention. The listener feels like they have been put on the spot and are forced to respond with more attentiveness. Because of this, the listener ensures to answer questions with care and detail.

Intimidation through the strength of numbers

An aggressor may want to intimidate another with a show of might and numbers. They take dominance of a situation by having their associates and friends present to reinforce their position. When the other party sees those numbers, they may get intimidated. In addition, his associates or friends can back each other up and occasionally challenge you during the process. In some instances, they will put undue pressure on you to make a decision before you feel ready to. At its worst, strength through numbers can be used to harass or bully an opponent directly or indirectly.

Uncomfortable formality

An aggressor may deliberately want to make their opponent uncomfortable and make them feel defensive. They do this by making their speech, physical environment, clothing and or the proceedings uncomfortable and formal. This feeling may be accurate if the formalities or demonstrations are not in accordance with their usual behavior.

When the aggressor is being excessively formal and extra, he or she may be trying to be impressive and psychologically intimidating in order to have an upper hand and get what they want from the proceedings.

They maintain an uncomfortable physical closeness to you

An aggressor may want to sit or stand uncomfortably close to you especially if they are taller to intimidate you with their height. When people stand tall over you, and uncomfortably close, naturally the height intimidates you. In so doing, the person hopes to gain a sense of superiority and psychologically dominate you to their advantage and at your expense.

They use procedure and red tape as a form of intimidation

Some people in an effort to show and maintain their position of power, they will use procedures, bureaucracy, by-laws and laws, paperwork, and much more to make it difficult for you. This technique is also used by those that want to delay those that are seeking facts or truth, to hide weaknesses and flaws or to avoid scrutiny.

Displaying negative emotion and using a raised voice

When holding a normal discussion, some aggressors will raise their voice to intimidate others. They believe that with raised voices and displaying negative emotions, you will yield to their coercion so that they get what they want. They often combine the aggressive voice with intimidating body language like using excited gestures or suddenly standing.

10. Threaten a walkout and lack of patience

Just like raising a voice, other power-play tactics that aggressors use to pressurize their listeners to conform are showing a lack of patience and threatening to walk out of a proceeding. If the recipient is emotionally invested in the situation or the aggressor, it gets easier for this kind of coercion to work on them.

11. Negative humor

An aggressor knows that using negative humor that focuses on your area of weakness will disempower you. He or she makes critical remarks disguised as humor to make their victim insecure and inferior. They can make negative comments about your appearance, your possessions like your phone or even your credentials and your background. By making a person feel and look bad, an aggressor hopes to psychologically impose their perceived superiority over you.

12. Constant criticism and judgment

An aggressor will make sure to criticize and judge your every move or decision so that you feel inadequate. In this case, the aggressor will directly pick on you. He or she will ridicule, marginalize and dismiss you to keep you off balance and have superiority over you. The aggressor wants you to think there is something wrong with you at all times and for the people around you to think the same. Regardless of how much you try, he or she works at making you feel nothing good can come out of you. At all times, they focus on your negative traits, but not once will they offer solutions that are constructive or helpful.

13. Pressurizing you to make a decision

This tactic is most common with salespeople. When a person wants you to buy something, they refuse to give you time to weigh your options and think through instead they want you to decide now. They apply tension and bully you into making a crucial decision without thinking through it. Even during negotiations, one party will put pressure on you to make a decision when you are not ready. They put undue pressure on you with the hope that you give in to their demands and they get their way without caring how you feel about the situation.

14. Giving you excessive and multiple directions

This is geared towards controlling you psychologically and behaviorally. This is a tactic common with law enforcers to control one's behavior. Individuals that like to control in business also use this tactic often. In domestic, intimate relationships and other situations, this tactic is also used by excessively controlling people. Some people use this tactic for no reason just because they want to bully and abuse their victims. They look at the vulnerability of their victims and take advantage of it.

15. Use of threats

Aggressors may use threats to intimidate their victims about the consequences that will come if they don't comply. The consequences are varied and can be emotional, legal, financial, psychological, physical, or social among others.

Difficult people that want to control others are everywhere. Knowing the tactics, they use is important for an individual so that you can use strategies available to restore respect and balance.

Why don't we realize it's happening?

Mind control is very difficult to detect. Those that use it are usually trusted, close people to use. They use subtle ways that the victim often believes they are responsible for their own decisions. Most mind control tactics are not physically aggressive. The aggressors also are careful in choosing their victims. Most of their victims are usually weak, vulnerable and in some cases, emotionally abused.

An individual that feels they need someone that loves them, believes in them and understands them are easy to manipulate this way. Studies indicate that most victims of mind control are individuals that have recently gone through a divorce, are ill, are undergoing a personal tragedy, their careers have failed, or are away from their loved ones and are lonely.

Many people that have been mentally controlled especially those in cults will never admit to it. They believe they made the decisions soberly and their leader is being targeted. Mind control can be so severe that their individuals choose their leader over their loved ones. These leaders use various tools to make their subjects loyal to them as discussed below.

Tools of mind control

Controlled environment – a manipulator or aggressor will make sure the victim is completely disconnected from their loved ones. They forbid any form of communication and brainwash them into thinking their family and friends are the enemies.

They break your sense of self – they attack their victim's self-esteem on the basis that they are wrong and their views are wrong as compared to the group is right.

They instill a new sense of self – the victim is given a new sense of identity, that of identifying with the group. This is reinforced by the group environment where the victim only interacts with members of the group and any information he or she gets is from the members. They train the victim on how to behave and the right way to live according to them.

1. Isolation – a victim is kept off the outside world. They are shunned from the internet or watching the news. Fear is instilled in

them such that they are afraid to venture out of the "safe" group environment.

Preventing Mind Control

- Ensure you maintain close contact with your family and friends

- Do not allow sulky or moody behavior from your partner control you

- Be on the lookout for nonverbal clues

- Refuse to agree with uncompromising rules

Conclusion

Now that you can recognize who the manipulators may be in your life (or whether you've been guilty of using these techniques as well), identify signs of being manipulated, and learn how to handle them, you can better evaluate the relationships around you to make the educated choices you need in your own life. Through a more realistic view of life, you may share your thoughts, opinions, and wishes without feeling guilty, realizing that they are indeed your own.

You can detect and understand persuasion and manipulation signals by evaluating and examining your relationships' contact signs. When that is evident, you will exercise your right to be treated with dignity. In a contact exchange, you regain the power and request to be equal individuals to yourself. In a relationship with an equal balance of control, you CAN say 'no' without feeling guilty and CAN set your goals to build a better life or world for yourself and others you care for.

The ability to interpret people's body language and see beyond misleading phrases stops you from being extorted or abused unknowingly. You are more open to opportunities around you and less likely to be affected by others' purpose and motivated by it. But being able to identify those tactics means that you too can manipulate these tricks. Be sure to consult with your moral compass and be always mindful of treating each person as an equal citizen, worthy of the right to be treated and free to choose.

The principle of Dark Psychology assumes you're ignorant of previous devious actions or just do not care. Here's an opportunity to change the trajectory of yours and start anew. Whatever predatory activities you've engaged in, criminal and sociopathic, there's usually a decision to cease, desist, and part from the abyss of getting sociopathic.

The head's capability might be said to be very vast, and this might be noted that the individuals that see how the mind of their functions might tend to get much more out of life. Additionally, learning how you can take control of the sense of yours might enable you to be in charge of the points that occur in daily life. Thus, rather than allowing life to come about for you, you can decide what goes on in the life of yours. The survivalist mentality is the norm of ours, and this what society tries to do is manage the wild beast in every man by teaching them out of an early age to obey the laws, morals, and rules of the controlling team, typically the rich, who dominate our institutions and governments.

Thus, must we condemn the ones that think society isn't providing them a fair offer - which they need to take whatever they have to endure an often hostile atmosphere in which privilege relies on the school of yours, wealth, or loved ones? Dark Psychology Secret itself needs to come out of the closet and acknowledge that the typical human action is opposing rules and societies strict.

The individuals resent society, but since they're powerless against people who control law-making and morality, they are helpless to live among the sheep.

On certain occasions, individuals take the responsibilities of creating a better society for themselves to enable a comfortable life free from external control from their communities. As we have seen, all eventual breakdown

All empires can't see the demise of theirs! Exactly how will Dark Psychology Secret then contend with this particular question of human behavior like a simple survivalist mechanism, in which humans are brutal, harsh, and dominating others that are weaker than themselves?

Psychiatry in mental hospitals is frequently viewed as an element of societal control. In case you are not coherent with society and the rules of it, you should be insane - for that reason, you need to be dedicated and managed for the security and the advantage of all.

On the other hand, dark psychology is viewed as the liberating part of psychological health - the place we help those out of synch with the society of finding the location of theirs and fit back into what's regarded behavior that is ordinary for that team.

Anywhere will the solution be for individuals who rebel against the society they live in and would like another method of presence without the interference of the practical and independence to live a life they select as suiting themselves. Or perhaps do we wait - for the films to come true the disaster that awaits a return, as well as all humans to a dog, called survivalism - the genuine cultural majority!

Around this junction, it's some time to determine from these observations which societal norms, laws, and morals are, in fact, "not normal" for man, and this society typically forces group conduct depending on what the highly effective want with the powerless.

Thank you for reading this book!